P9-DEN-859

MARGIE

The American Journal of Poetry

VOLUME TWO

*Editor-&-*Chief
ROBERT NAZARENE

Publisher
MARGARET S. LAWTER

Senior Editor
JAMES WILSON

Web Design
THOMAS D. WILSON

Special Projects
MONA FRAME

Ethics & Policy Advisor
Sister ANNA R. TREBORZE

MARGIE / The American Journal of Poetry, is published in the fall of the year by MARGIE, Inc., Post Office Box 250, Chesterfield, MO 63006-0250. Web Address: www.margiereview.com. Upon publication, all rights for individual works revert to the authors. The opinions and points of view expressed in this review are solely those of the individual authors.

The Marjorie J. Wilson Award for Excellence in Poetry is awarded annually. First Prize: $2,500, and publication for best poem. Guidelines for the Award are available at our website or by sending a self-addressed, stamped envelope to our mailing address: PO Box 250, Chesterfield, MO 63006-0250. Deadline for *The Marjorie J. Wilson Award for 2004* is March 31, 2004. Contest Judge for the forthcoming competition is Charles Simic, winner of the Pulitzer Prize in Poetry.

MARGIE publishes superlative poetry without restriction to form, school or subject matter. A distinctive voice is prized. MARGIE's hallmark is STRONG MEDICINE.

SUBMISSIONS: Unsolicited submissions are accepted during our open reading period from June 1st-October 15th each year. SUBSCRIBERS ONLY may submit poetry at any time of the year. Mark "Subscriber" on the outside of your submission envelope, please. Please submit between 3-5 poems with your name, address, phone and email (if possible) on each poem. All submissions should be mailed to: MARGIE / The American Journal of Poetry at PO Box 250, Chesterfield, MO 63006-0250. PLEASE NOTE: S.A.S.E. must accompany all submissions to receive a response. No fax or email submissions. MARGIE is a writer-friendly review. Every effort will be made to answer your submission within 30 days' time, sooner if possible. Simultaneous submissions are acceptable. Please send copies only, not originals, as poems will not be returned. A cover letter and bio are desirable, although not necessary. MARGIE is open to publishing newer and established poets, equally.

MARGIE / The American Journal of Poetry is available by Subscription Only. Annual subscription rates are: $11.95 Individuals (one issue) and $16.95 Institutions & Outside US (one issue).

.www.margiereview.com *(Please visit our website often for news of upcoming features, events, and excerpts from the review.)*

COVER ART: Courtesy of The Missouri Historical Society, St. Louis.
Catching the Wild Horse, plate 4, North American Indian Portfolio, deluxe ed. Artist: George Catlin, lithograph (1844).

Indexed by the INDEX OF AMERICAN PERIODICAL VERSE (Lanham, MD: Scarecrow Press).

"no time ago". Copyright 1950, © 1978, 1991 by the Trustees for the E. E. Cummings Trust. Copyright © 1979 by George James Firmage, from COMPLETE POEMS: 1904-1962 by E. E. Cummings, edited by George J. Firmage. Used by permission of Liveright Publishing Corporation.

First Edition   © Copyright 2003 by MARGIE, Inc.

ISSN 0-9719040-0-6   Library of Congress Control Number 2002107173

Dedicated to the Spirit and Memory of

MARJORIE J. WILSON
(1955-1977)

With Love

M A R G I E
The American Journal of Poetry
STRONG MEDICINE

VOLUME ONE
SOLD OUT!
(from "concept" to *collector's item*...)

"Bravo! Not since the launch of *Antaeus*
many years ago can I recall a new poetry
magazine featuring such a breadth of different and significant talent.

> --Robert Farnsworth, poetry
> editor, *The American Scholar*

"The first issue of Margie is a poetry feast...With
such excellent editing there will be many more
fine issues to come."

> --T. Alan Broughton

"A sterling anthology-journal."
> --Fred Chappell

"Strong Medicine indeed...So many amazing poets
& poems...this yearly book is a prize in itself. Many
thanks to the stellar "tribal council" for this fantastic
work."

> --Literary Magazine Stand, *New Pages*

"*Margie* is indeed Strong Medicine. However various the voices, these are poems that are moving, necessary."

--Margaret Gibson

"…a journal worth keeping & living with…"

--X.J. Kennedy

"Margie is a marvel-a meeting ground for all the voices in poetry today."

--Jesse Lee Kercheval

"…terrific debut issue—sign me up for a subscription—Robert, you really do things right—"

--Ronald Wallace

"Margie bursts on the scene filled with some of the most lively, eclectic and mind-opening poems anywhere to be found."

--Dara Wier

THE MEDICINE LODGE

CONTENTS
OF
THE SECOND VOLUME

FOREWORD

no time ago
or else a life
walking in the dark
i met christ

jesus)my heart
flopped over
and lay still
while he passed(as

close as i'm to you
yes closer
made of nothing
except loneliness

---E. E. Cummings

ABU BAKR

Admonition
(translated by Richard O'Connell)

Be on your guard against all men:
Keep a sharp eye and a keen sword.
Consider no one a true friend.
Befriend a preying wolf, but flee
Before an open-seeming man.
Walk wary in the daggered world.

DICK ALLEN

Unrelenting Fear

I keep being hounded by that image of Larry Levis
on the Ohio Poetry Circuit,
not wanting to do anything but read and write
as the shadows come around him,
and that lonely Holiday Inn out on Interstate 70,
the rooms with their tolerable paintings,
where Levis, drug-worn,
holds a small orange notebook as he paces and sets on blue lines
his last terrible fragments,
and how, twenty miles away, in New Concord, Ohio
(birthplace of John Glenn),
everything's what it should be on an autumn night,
the supper good, the television good, the sex good,
America so contented with how it is in the late 1980s,
who'd long for elsewhere. But Levis keeps thinking
What is it? What is it?
as he places in his notebook…
fire,
a child's head,
from somewhere irresolute, magnolias,
and a half dozen thumbtacks lying on their sides.
Thought's needles and pins, he says aloud,
the doors of a stranger. He remembers
the moon above New Concord through the elms
and something his host had said, after the reading,
about a river of poets that flowed through here,
all nodding and bobbing,
amusing, amused
(through New Concord, Ohio,
birthplace of John Glenn),
and now Levis is angry
at all he's done to himself and others,
most of his life gone up in imaginings,

22

the life of a poet, goddamn it, goddamn your eyes,
then wouldn't you know it,
it's raining outside. Through the window,
incredible streaks of rain divide the night
while out on the Interstate,
the highbeams flick to life the road that vanishes
east to West Virginia, west to God knows where.

ERIC ANDERSON

The Personal

If you're Phoebe, I love you. I promise you,

I'm familiar with the Supreme.

I have such good scars; should you want

what is best, there's only one person.

How can I fight? If you have reservations,

I understand. I have no job prospects.

I may rearrange, slightly alter, swap parts.

I know I never try anything. I wish I could

wear skimpy clothes, make suggestive remarks.

I want to change, so I tinker with myself

but I'm tired. I'm throwing

a goodbye party for myself,

I wish you would come. I'm holding

my sacred memory, my flammable shrine,

a thousand tiny tablets.

If you love, overflow. I overflow.

SHERI ANDERSON

David and Linda

Things are done differently,
The way tuna salad is fixed
Or Oreos are eaten,
The way he loves her
Is startling to most,
Annoying.
One could wish,
Hope,
Pray
She would leave
Do better.
Do different.
He looks and speaks
Indirectly
As if she isn't present
Or her presence is,
As Eeyore would say,
A bother. While he's reading
The newspaper, he'll grunt,
Which obviously means I love you,
I hate you, You stink, Your mama.
He'll speak of a movie that might be good
Which means I want to
Spend time with you or I want to
Get away from you.
She catches what she can,
Her reach often not long enough,
For this,
The love of her life.

JULIANNA BAGGOTT

Q and A: What do you do with poems that don't work?

I've never burned them or bundled them with ribbon
to cast over an iron bridge rail.
I let them sit, a punishment, and they disengage.
Some wander off to be raised by wolves, by chickens,
once I heard of a poem living in a bee hive
and the poem was never stung.
                  Those that remain, drawer-ful,
can turn to seamstress chalk, a thick caulk,
      can shift sometimes into
a firecracker, a Ferris wheel, a spider,
slim-legged, pale green
        picking its way from a flower's
            widening, many tongued-mouth.

JULIANNA BAGGOTT

Q and A: Are you afraid of writer's block?

Wouldn't it be the same as when my neck seizes
and I cannot bow my head

or check my back for the shuffling gunman?
Those stiff mornings I cannot stare at the sky

to decide just when the heavy clouds will burst.
And Jesus, I'm finally free of him,

unable to search each passing face
for the pained weight of his cross.

Friends don't recognize me,
erect and purposeful, suddenly proud, fearless,

on equal footing with the world.
Breathless with pain, I am almost happy.

JEFFERY BAHR

Past Lives Pavilion

He's the one who braids the hair of the dead
and lowers them into the bog. Sometimes
they let him keep a cape or a bracelet.
This one's the woman of Gwrtheyrn.

Here he is, ducking the hunt, scraping hides
until his nails break, then chewing the stiff
leather. Another of the tribe returns
on a travois with a bloody calf, visible tibia.

He had one black boil just below his groin
but survived by the kindness of his sister.
Eight years later, he marries her off for four
guinea fowl and a pair of gloves.

He has kept to his vows and mastered illumination:
Blanche of Castile and her son Saint Louis.
He instructs his scribes to place his small figure beneath
the King's feet as the iconographer of Revelations.

The Highlanders manage to complete their formation
trapping the French cavalry, killing them all.
He is the orderly who risks his position by whispering
to Ney that his plan was impeccable.

He hired the boy who threw the bomb
in Haymarket, then had him silenced.
Pinkerton approves and he goes on to plan
the murders at Homestead, the hanging of the Mollies.

He gets on his knees and prays with the Quaker.
The President asks him how things have gone wrong

(no stanza break)

28

and cries as he strikes his fist on the carpet, which
Henry notices is a fine example of Meskabad artistry.

THERESA DEVINE BANFORD

Home from Vietnam

You came back.
That first night, we sat
at my mother's table,
covered in New England lace.
Five of us: three sisters and a friend,
and you, with your hair too short,
your oxford shirt from high school,
your new jeans—too stiff, too blue.

We were strangers.
Braless in our gauzy shirts,
long hair loosened from tight flips.
Peace signs around our necks,
in our ears.
Smug in our new selves.

We learned the war
flaunting black armbands
in high school, from protests
on our expensive college campuses,
between spring break and new sweaters.

All night you pulled at the lace,
loosening the threads.

What did we know
of the smell of a village burning?
Of foxholes
or the beauty of the moon above gunfire?
Tagging bodies.
The fear of looking scared,
of not making it home,
making it home.
The tyranny of fog.

HADARA BAR-NADAV

Gravity

In the same drunken sentence
Beth claimed to hate birds
and her profile

as if the two converged—
feathers and claws with the curve
of her nose and chin.

I've seen a bird's shadow
before the bird itself,
a thin moment when its sleek form

pauses between my head
and the sun, slides across
the macadam, and flies up

the side of a house,
disappearing over the roof.
Beth too wished her silhouette

dissolved at the top of the sky.
She saw it pinned to the street.

HADARA BAR-NADAV

The Last Gesture

My hand grew big as a house.
It was heavy to carry
and drag through the streets.

I staggered across the lawn
on gravel-burned knees
to watch the home
I could no longer enter.

My wrung wrist turned blue.
My shoulder bled.
Skin tore up my neck
and split open my eye.

I had given too much.
I had taken too much.

The hand grew
as the sky grew,
hand the size of wind

expanding until it was no longer
my own, until the weight
buried me.

HADARA BAR-NADAV

Dismissed

I keep the list in a three-ring binder.
I compile it late at night at the dog food plant
and keep it locked in my desk,
the key hidden in an old snow boot.

My wife whose breath smells of another man's semen is on the list.
My son who smokes pot in the basement is on the list.
My daughter who will not speak, but cries loudly.
My mother who died and left me her sinking house.
The house with its walls and roof wrinkling with rot.
The lawn with its dead grass and cotton-headed weeds
and the law ordering me to mow it all down.

I want to strip off my clothes on the front lawn in daylight.
I want the sun to burn me into the ground.

J. T. BARBARESE

The Boy on His Father's Shoulders

The world's a slut, the mind's a slum
that slumbers through this smart parade.

Look at him, on the shoulders of
his picked giant. Slicked head popped

out of his white communion suit,
wet as a hatchling

his Buster Browns on the old man's chest,
his face scrubbed, sweet neck shaved,

eyes lording it over the parked-up street
he fords like a child god.

WALTER BARGEN

Yours? Mine?

Now, and sometimes daily,
in other fields, someone
simply headed in the wrong direction,
a step here, there, distracted, by the moon,

the play of goats, a neighbor shouting a warning,
and someone rises up dead or surprised, if there's time,
foot missing, calf shredded,
leg ripped away

at the knee, the hip, the splintered
bones driven up into the lungs,
embedded in the ragged, raging stump,
stone and dirt missiled through genitals,

the single-minded mine
a kind of diminished birth,
exploding into the rest of someone's life,
never getting back up.

COLEMAN BARKS

Good as Dead

With my deli sandwich I sometimes sit under a big
        poster of B.B.
                King, eyes almost closed, cheek

resting on his hands folded over the headstock where
        the tuning pegs are.
                There's a rectangular jeweled shield

on the left ring finger and a prongheld bezel on his
        left little. The guitar
                neck inlaid with mother-of-pearl says *Lucille,*

the woman who calls in ocean detail for the turtleskin
        back of his hands. Strong
                silver steel strings stretch down and

off the bottom waiting to be told BE   BE   We wait as
        music makes us wait, as
                good as dead. Hello honeypot. My friend

Seawright comes in dream to a live friend Debi to tell
        her to tell me he's
                fine; *happy* the word used, which when

living I never knew him to. She leaves the message on my
        machine. Surely the here
                and the gone converse. Listen to the clock

of this fire-ticking woodpop white pine, two old women, Miss
        Williams and Miss Rhodes, how
                they brought three trees from North

Carolina that Henry Girard has cut down and rather than haul
        away, the two men split
                and stack for me for $50. This is

the material plane where logrings spun into smoke get paid
        for with wordpaper tossed
                in. I have heard the Buddha was sitting

with a group near the end of his life. He said you may ask
        me anything except there must
                be nothing about God, the soul, liberation,

death, love, the transmission of light, peace, desire, the
        mystery of the blessed
                one, suffering, enlightenment, or what

it means to die before you die. I pick a cellophane
        redstripe cigar
                wrapping-opener from the step in front

of me. Nearly napping, I am sweeping the twelve
        backstairs with an image
                behind the sunlight delighting

my eyes, of a woman with bare breasts, white
        silk sliding across.

TONY BARNSTONE

A Bowl of Bean Soup

"You don't know anything," he hears her snap
through the screen door, out on the patio,
smoking. She says, "Why can't he let me go?"
He holds a bowl of bean soup on his lap.
When his sister'd called, he'd said, "You talk,"
"I don't know what to say to her," gave up
the phone and sat down with his soup. He shuts
his eyes and forces a few bites, then stops.
His stomach is too tight. Great soup, no meat,
three kinds of bean, with corn and carrots, but
he can't go on. To live you have to eat.
Why do you have to live? The beans are hot
and something tight inside begins to give.
One spoon. Another. This is how you live.

TONY BARNSTONE

Plans for the Future

She watches as he signals to the waiter.
He doesn't notice how she's silent now,
he doesn't see her sadness, can't see how
her eyes go dark and still as stagnant water.
Behind them in a fluid tangle, strange
ideas are coiled, involute, entwined,
like eels. She watches how the subtle wind
tears at her husband's hat. It isn't strong
enough to toss it to the sky, but tugs
and grabs and shakes and doesn't stop. Perhaps
a hurricane is needed. What she hopes:
a bomb will drop, all things will die but bugs,
the continent will slip into the sea,
the planet will implode, and she'll be free.

STEVEN BARZA

Interior Clues II

The secret face of the word
has been peering out of the word
all along.
The agenda is there, blazing
in letters, like the remnant
of a partially burned out
neon sign.

There's ex in exercise and exhibition
because a former love is ever hovering,
ever driving the sweat and directing the show.

There's rig in trigger,
because every catalyst is a complex
contraption of hinges, levers, pulleys.

There's treat in retreat
because alone one can treat oneself
exactly as one pleases.

There's bell in rebellion.
There's volt in revolt.
There's mother in smother.
There's imp in impartial.
There's ruth in truth.

There's less in blessing
than some people think,
than some people hop and beg and pray for.

AMY BEEDER

Photo of M. Pasteur

Pestilence his coin: this glaring Frenchman,
sixty-four with tie askew
berating his assistant Emile Roux—arrogant, brash

he put his head into the circlets of poison
entered willingly chapels of bacilli
inhabited also fully the sadness of certain hours

dearest Marie so they will all die, our dear children
waited long moments for the sheep
to rise from Rossignol's pasture & stumble

from dawn fog & the scourge of charbon (but cried
from the train: *So, men of little faith!*)
Up to his neck in beet-juice & the favor of chance

with a crook-neck flask, the man who, attending a lecture
on childbed fever at the Paris Academy
sprung up impatient, shouting

then drew for them in chalk the *streptococcus*
a string of bead he'd seen shine under his lens
like the eggs of a toad painted scarlet.

AARON BELZ

Henry the Eighth

I.

I sat with my head sort of hanging—in the tiled atrium.
I sat in the tiled atrium—with my head sort of hanging.
In the tiled atrium I sat with my head hanging—sort of.

Sort of hanging my head I sat in the tiled atrium.
I sat sort of hanging my head in the tiled atrium.

Buffalo cheese, buffalo cheese. Buffalo cheese.

I sat with my head sort of hanging—in the tiled atrium.

II.

III.

IV.

She sat in the wide gondola, its colorful hood
playing gaily in the breeze.

In the wide gondola she sat in the breeze playing
gaily its colorful hood.

Henry James.

V.

VI.

Monster cheese, monster cheese, we sculpt our monster cheese.

VII.

As we went, however, in her gondola,
gliding there under the sociable hood
with the bright Venetian picture framed on either side

    by the movable window,

I could see that she was amused by my infatuation.

VIII.

Henry the Eighth.

F. J. BERGMANN

In the Final Analysis

The man who hates himself
wanders on the dark hillside,
waiting for the lean blessing of moonrise.
He wonders how others feel about him,
is certain as to how he feels
about himself.

The man who hates himself
weeps in the night. He imagines
the trickles filling twisted
fissures of malformed stone
stained with oxides; palomino to blue,
canyon shadow to gold.

The man who hates himself
always thinks he should be somewhere else,
be someone kinder or more useful,
know how to carve a decoy, a mask,
how to embroider. Perhaps he could learn to
swallow swords.

The man who hates himself
reads the books of others who also
hate themselves. He wants to believe that
the next page, or the next, will tell him
why they do this, what makes them
take the blame.

The man who hates himself
leaves footprints that sprout with green
herbs as each sole lifts, coltsfoot, chamomile,
the miniature comfort of thyme. He never looks

(no stanza break)

over his shoulder, never crosses
his own past.

When the fog moves in
he can no longer tell whether
the path is ascending
or angled downward.
The moon's gift
is silence.

EDWARD BOCCIA

Laying It On Thick

I am Carlos,
painter of eyes and noses,
creator of lips and necks, maker
of the whole figure.
Edmundo is my middle name, he who
manipulates body parts,
the blender of skin and bone.
The only artist west of the Mississippi
who washes his hands in turpentine.
The only painter whose full name
is Carlos Edmundo Frankenstein,
he who makes people come alive with paint,
the only composer of still lives
that grow out of their frames.

Come to my studio some day.
I have racks full of nudes
and half dressed fools.
I have portfolios jammed with sketches
of squares and triangles. So what
if I call the triangles *love*
and the squares *hate*.
I am Carlos,
blender of opposites,
Carlos the peace maker.
Come, take off your clothes
and confess your sins. If I like
what I see, I'll paint you.
If I like what I hear,
I'll frame you.

EDWARD BOCCIA

Revenge of the Yard Bird

I am not a squirrel,
my friends are not birds.
I do not have a tail
nor am I accustomed
to eating nuts.
Certain members of my family have a red spot
behind their necks; two of them are uncles
who are so old they don't remember the war.
I do have an aunt
who talks about her first husband
as if he is still alive,
but then she has a growth on her ear
which makes her look like a hen
that's had better days.
My cousin Latitia chirps,
but not like a canary
and my son-in-law tries to tap his fingers
in time with the song the robin sings,
except he misses a beat now and then.
I remember my platoon sergeant, years ago,
who never missed a beat
squawking like a jay bird into my ear.
I remember how red his face got,
the crazy way he swung his arms
and when we were overseas
where the bullets were flying,
I remember exactly
how I killed him.

DEBORAH BOGEN

Home Movies

The shape of the head which
you see from the backseat of the Buick,
a corona of smoke and a roll of fat
above the stiff white collar.

Then the lap where you sink into "Black Beauty",
more smoke, a watch ticking.

Later, sled runners on snow,
a man pulling you, the long coat and hat
        make him look like
all the other fathers.

His eyes stare right into yours,
        but you can't really remember that.

        ~

Later, normal life,
everything according to a carpenter's square.

You think of him skating under
a street light,

and the Fourth of July when
he put you on his shoulders and galloped
across the dark lawns.

        ~

This is Red Lodge.

(no stanza break)

Your horse is Duchess, a golden horse,
a big gold horse. The man
on the brown horse
is Daddy.
    His back's wet.
This is a good place.
He brought you here, drove you up

the Going-to-the-Sun Road.

'   ~

You must be fourteen when
you find him slumped in the autumn gold
recliner,
        the bourbon gone,
medical books splayed across his lap.

He reads to learn what it means,
this prognosis.
        Is he bathed in the lamplight?

            ~

And when he dies,
when he sets the car ablaze to end it,
        amnesia.

The need to wander out into the blizzard,
        into snow,
                with its anti-convulsant effects,
without obligatory electrical activity.

Without memory,
        or lack of memory.

            ~

Then somehow you're grown.
      Your mother's come to see your kids.
Before she leaves, she says
     I thought you might want this,

hands you the can heavy with film,
"Whitefish Lake, 1959".
     That was the summer you learned
to ski, Dad in the boat facing back to film it.

He's got you dipping into rough water,
but later he shifts his aim to the shoreline,

     tree, after tree, after tree, after tree.

And he can't get enough of it.

GERRY BOLAND

beyond the farmyard gate

The signs are ominous.
In flat fields
near farmhouses
clouds of sheep have formed.
Yesterday
sheep dogs brought
with masterly flair thousands
down the tricky hills.

They stand and wait
for whatever lies
beyond the farmyard gate.

Soon
yesterday's panic will pale
amid the shouting and the barking
the falling on the fouled ramp
the breathless cramming
in the semi-darkness
of the transport truck.
Into their nostrils will sink
the sour stench of the slaughterhouse
suffocating memories of hillside heather.

SUSAN BRENNAN

Afternoon Bomb

On a test field, her husband will rush the ash.
In the meantime, the bottom of a copper pan
soaks, dishwater thins, kids roll in the grass.
Why, she asked him last August,
do we still need to test, since all the Japs are dead?
His answer was short, unsatisfying.

She met Mr. Oppenheimer at a military party.
She wanted to sound interesting, she meant to be funny,
confessing her private game of seeing the lady in the bomb.
He took her to a side room, his hand cold on her forearm.
He was handsome, had won history's assurance.
A woman's face in the bomb—Margaret, are you sure?
Yes, with lush eyelashes and a sad full mouth.

She rounds up the children for a photo.
Her husband promised this afternoon's bomb
would be something special. Margaret waits
at the kitchen window, the glass reflects her face
her Hawthorn red lips lay over the bouffant explosion
and she is the Atomic Lady of Nevada.
She holds up two palm-fulls of suds.

After all, science has given her
so many products, plenty of time to herself.
In the baby's room, the wallpaper shrinks,
tightens. Does lick the ears of their fawns
on an infinite pink background.
I wonder if all those babies are all right.
She catches herself.

At the party, she had met the other one too,
with the crazy hair. He smelt foreign,
reminded her of the Mad Hatter,
filling his tea cup, keeping it hot
I would have been a watch maker,
if only I had known.

drea brown

gray wall

forty seven blac faces

behind orange suits steel bracelets

lockin us bothers

reminds me of my mother

less self who never knew mother never knew mother never knew

    mother never knew

mother so mammy never knew no language

has no tongue to tongue down to me

liberate me lover

I am stuc

    right here.

between the memories of nine-year-old gyrl queens split w i d e

    open

in church house s basement s thirteen and fourteen late nite bruises

sleeping with knife under pillow

am i so abnormal

or just remembering too much

weary

       ness

yes

i am

          weary

       mother

less

self

is almost in visible

       and tha thic grayness is all

but memory is

foundation.

We are pleased to announce results for

The St. Louis Poetry Center Award
for 2003

FIRST PRIZE: $2,000 & Publication
(Contest Judge: JAMES TATE)
is awarded to:

"God Bless Our Crop-Dusted
Wedding Cake"
by:

ASHLEY CAPPS
of Charlotte, North Carolina

2nd Prize: GEORGE LOONEY, Erie, PA

3rd Prize: JOHN HODGEN, Shrewsbury, MA

FINALISTS

ALLISON JOSEPH, Carbondale, IL
GARY T. LEISING, Cincinnati, OH
R. A. PAVOLDI, Schenectady, NY
JACQUELINE SHAH, Houston, TX
DEREK SHEFFIELD, Home, WA
TOM SMITH, Castleton, VT
NICOLE WALKER, Salt Lake City, UT

ASHLEY CAPPS

God Bless Our Crop-Dusted Wedding Cake

When my mother lifted her shirt
to show the sunken grave of her breast,
the fresh tarantula tattoo she'd chosen

over reconstruction, I shuddered at first.
The last bad joke she'd play on her body—
chest half-spider, fanged, half-planetary:

lone red nipple circling itself like Jupiter's
perpetual storm—and I but spectator
to so much bad weather. Like summer

1967, when she roped me to the pier,
when I was ten and she was drunk in her bikini
and wanted to watch the hurricane come in.

The green sky spun like an automated car-wash!
Acorn barnacles oatmealed my back, a population
of lobsters blew past like the rusty contents of a toolbox.

Dad took one look at my rope-burns and punched her.
But Mom wore her bruises like high art, her broken
nose a study in cubism, blue flowers blooming

under her skin like watercolor.
But there were times we acted like a family.
Dad came home with a telescope and we watched the stars

fall into the ocean like broken teeth.
We sipped Jim Beam from muscular tea-cups,
channeled my grandmother who finally showed up

in her bank-robber uniform, sweet smile pig-faced
through the stocking, but dear nonetheless.
Ours was the best-dressed scare-crow,

in Dad's bowling shirt and Mom's peek-a-boo
lace thong. The landscape was wrong for birds
but it kept Jehovah's Witnesses away. Which is

not to say we never prayed. When my mother knelt
I could hear her rattle-snake rattler earrings
chatter like rosary beads in the darkness. She prayed

for my sister to take the For Sale sign off
of her body and come home to sleep in a new pair
of soft pajamas. My sister could not.

*

So while it is true she has cleared the atmosphere celestial, left me
gravity-strapped and mourning, blistered through cloud cover,

while she has gifted me one schizoid father's government-issue
ashes, one grey-eyed sister's prostitute bones, a brief family

history in cardboard, percussive teeth and my double helix
    permanently scarred;
while it is true she daily christened the oarless boat of my
    childhood,

she never broke a single bottle against me.
So if my mom shows up in her ghost bikini with both breasts
    intact and a lasso

chasing my neck through a sandstorm, I'll let her.
I'll hand her a beer and watch my huge flip flops fly off in the
    wind.

ALAN CATLIN

Dress Rehearsal for the Village of the Damned on Quail Street

The advance scout is a young
man afflicted by muscular con-
tractions, lurching as he walks,
each unmeasured, hesitant step
an adventure in imbalance: spastic
tics, gnarled fingers useless except
for signing a mute's language
of the damned. His companions,
comrades-at-arms, congregate
dead center of the sidewalk,
napalming charcoal with firestarter,
that stuff that comes in squeezable
cans they squirt, two at a time,
thrilled to the core by the singular
rush of Hibachi bbq emitting
tracer type rounds, chemicals already
past the point of ignition, launching
them toward the source, the hands and
faces of the watchers transformed
from zombie like spacing cadets
to a manic glee fueled by warm
malt liquors, synthetic drugs, magic
mushrooms and the weird glow
of their communal flesh roasting pyres
as their spawn play hide and go seek
games, scattering in all directions,
running out from between parked
cars without looking. The ones too
crippled for playing, the mentally
deficients, stand, curbside holding

(no stanza break)

60

limp jump ropes they cannot begin
to comprehend how to use, stand
mystified, clogging the walkways
with their elders, those former pathways
made impassable now to all but
the most intrepid, the most determined
of the walkers who proceed with their eyes
averted, holding their hand carved wooden
crosses extended as they come,
nervously clutching strung garlic necklaces,
hoping the sound of the savage fluttering
of wings overhead is only a brace
of pigeons being chased from squalid building
ledges, eaves, by smoke clouds and flames.
The sound of their frantic, deep wheezing
breath is like that of the damned ones
consigned to iron lungs for the duration
of their terminal diseases, smoke ringed
layers of hell; the smell of burnt flesh,
stale beer and animal waste more than man
was meant to bear.

BARBARA DILTZ CHANDLER

Inheritance

Plump marionberries,

flour and butter,

tapioca,

cinnamon and nutmeg.

It's her cobbler I'm baking,

her flavors I blend,

her curt verbs I obey.

My predecessor's,

the deceased.

I'm the next wife

who never knew her,

exhuming the stiff wooden box,

the hushed cards

precisely printed by a steady hand

years before breast cancer

and now,

years after.

JAN CLAUSEN

The Straits

Swim
and you are not in your country.—*Richard Hugo*

1.
It's always
been
about edges

snowberry
Nootka
rose

stranded
kelp orgies
fly-visited

some collective
swerve of
sea life

12,000 years
since glaciers
took a powder

old beaches
hoisted
above us

sandy
birdy
autumn sedgy

lichen fruiting
all over
island rock

madrone's
fall fettle
blazing like Malinche

sunlight dragging
a pale sleeve
across bluffs

Pacific
rimming
the skyboys

2.
afternoon in an
SUV with relatives
chasing the elemental

talk out here's
of Costco
and toxins

cloperylid
sushi trays and
creosote

drunk Seattle
mothers hunkered down
in the 1950's

"I almost got
a goat in
San Francisco"

Dick Hugo's wave-
stopped bleak
gussied with gadgets

RV's called Lakota
rigged
for satellite

days of
advection fog
and gorgonzola

to each
white town its
"friendly" Indian

"so many fish
right now people
getting kinda crazy"

where's nature
are we
there yet

3.
world comes down
with its dark
over diligence

all falls
let it fall
away west

singly kindle
land lamps
and sea lamps

up Whidbey
and whale-
raked Haro

a fool
and his folly
are soon

leader
follow
the breath

it's always
been
about edges

old cold salt
inhuman
tides

those great
liquid
roads

if you
like
difficulty

JAN CLAUSEN

Critter

East

Beside a pond chartreuse with algae
like indoor-outdoor carpeting,

the sinewy cyclist gripped a ringing fish—
no: a silvery cell phone.

~

"Pacific Northwest? It must be
beautiful out there."

~

Did somebody mention
a visit to Shark Cathedral?

~

I'll tear you apart like a fish,
yelled Franz's father.

West

Drift limbs ricked in the old way.
Cold beach   foggy gravel.

Tide currents drive
like a river in that sea.

Ocean self   tree self.
Anadromous hecatombs.

I'll tear you apart like a fish,
yelled Franz's father.

~

18, 20 whalewatch boats
per orca.

A job or a critter?
Which?

~

Clubbing hatchery salmon
on the Methow

from a pristine
point of view.

~

Stumped? Just cuff
yourself to the mast

and chant: coho/aluminum
coho/aluminum.

At tether's end, inquire:
What would Kafka do?

Note: The line "I'll tear you apart like a fish" is from Kafka's "Letter to his
Father."

DAVID CLEWELL

My Father's Less-Than-Celebrated Feud with Orson Welles

Incredible as it may seem, both the observations of science and the evidence of our eyes lead to the inescapable conclusion that those strange beings who landed in the Jersey farmlands tonight are the vanguard of an invading army from the planet Mars.

> --from the so-called "Panic Broadcast," Orson Welles and the Mercury Theatre's radio adaptation of H.G. Wells' *War of the Worlds*

It went back to Grovers Mill, New Jersey, 1938, the night
before Halloween, when that first unlikely cylinder came down
and the Martians climbed out, rose up high on their metal tripods
and cut loose with those otherworldly heat rays on this Mischief Night
gone horribly wrong for the human race. Or so my father thought—
for a few hours longer than he liked to admit, even decades later.
When he first heard that Martians had landed a scant half-hour away
from his twice-mortgaged house in New Brunswick, he thought maybe
    this
would be the fiery end of the world. He'd never heard of H.G. Wells or
Orson Welles or the Mercury Theatre on the Air. But surely
no one would cut in on a live rendition of *Stardust*—Ramon Raquello
and his orchestra from the Meridian Room of the fabulous Park Plaza
    Hotel—
unless whatever breaking story was the kind that needed telling in a
    hurry.

And he couldn't wait to hear what on Earth was happening next.
The country had barely clambered out of the Depression
when the jitters over another world at war set in.
He lived by the radio in 1938, doing his best to keep up with Hitler
and Mussolini and Chamberlain on their way to the shaky Munich Pact,
    with
every one of FDR's smoky exhalations—*chats*, the President made a
    point
of calling them, although they were scripted, one-sided conversations.
My father retained an unwavering faith in what he called, simply, *the news*

in this storied year of the Lone Ranger, Snow White, and Superman.
The New York Yankee juggernaut had flattened the Cubs in four
    straight.
And my father stayed tuned to the radio. He listened to everything,
    hard,
trying to sort out the annual conflation of supposed villains and heroes.

                          *****

And on that night, shortly after 8, all the free-floating fear in the air
came in for what felt like an unmistakably solid landing
outside a tiny farm town, POP. 200, chosen at random
when scriptwriter Howard Koch closed his eyes and brought his pencil
    down
on the gas-station map spread out across his desk. And there, just
    barely,
was Grovers Mill, almost lost in the shadow of Princeton—an Ivy-
    League town
my father always disparaged in his telltale workingman's way:
They think they're so smart in Princeton. But Grovers Mill,
and what was about to unfold, would never be quite so unheard of
    again.
For years after the broadcast, one enterprising farmer posted a sign: *50¢*
FOR A WALK THROUGH THE FIELD WHERE THOSE THINGS
    FROM OUTER SPACE CAME DOWN,
GUARANTEED! because such visits were rare and truly alien then,
    before
the post-war Age of Flying Saucers, before *The Day the Earth Stood Still,*
before the universal willies of Conspiracy and sinister Government
    Cover-up.
And for the rest of his life, my father would go miles out of his way
just to avoid Grovers Mill. Until Orson Welles,
he used to drive right through it, not even knowing it was there.

                          *****

If only he'd been listening from the beginning, he wouldn't have missed
the announcer's introduction of "the director and star of these
    broadcasts,
Orson Welles." But he was switching from the rival *Chase and Sanborn*
    Hour,
where Edgar Bergen and Charlie McCarthy—the bright stars of Sunday
    night—
had just yielded the mike to some godawful singer my father had no

time for.
He tuned in for the weekly antics, the cockeyed joy he never questioned:
a ventriloquist on radio.
                              If only he'd hung on longer once he'd got
    there—
past the mock news bulletins, the on-location reporting that reminded
    him how,
by accident, he'd heard one of the first eyewitness news reports ever
when the *Hindenburg* caught fire over Lakehurst, New Jersey the year
    before—
he would have found this havoc clearly staged, unleashed from a studio
on the twentieth floor of CBS, New York.
                                    Or if he'd somehow thought
to change stations again, listening for what anyone else on the scene
was trying desperately to describe, he might have lucked back into
a triumphant dummy's latest wooden zinger or, less happily,
might have discovered Nelson Eddy nevertheless warbling away, and
    surely
he would have conceded: everything's still mostly right with the world.

Common sense would have suggested there wasn't time enough for this.
The creatures had left Mars, landed on Earth, deployed the invasion,
and completed the takeover in the unlikely space of forty-five minutes.
But common sense had been eclipsed by the darker, more exotic
power of Martian suggestion. And either way he looked at it,
the problem was real: everything was happening so goddamn fast.
My father could hear neighbors crying on their porches,
the sound of car horns, motors revving up and down the long block.

                            *****

He never lost control entirely—a sinking feeling in his stomach,
yes, but he was not about to join the tumult in the streets.
He'd do his level best to stay cool, even under interplanetary fire.
Maybe he was thinking, seriously, if the Martians make it to New
    Brunswick,
he might not have to pay the butcher's bill. He was that determined
to be more or less himself—and damn the cataclysm.
                                        At least he'd
    never be
the woman calling the bus-lines for information: *Please hurry.*
The world is coming to an end, and I have a lot to do.
He wasn't closing windows and turning out the lights
as if the Martians were distant relatives hitting town without warning

71

and could so easily be fooled into thinking no one's home. He wasn't
the preacher suddenly frozen in his holy tracks at the pulpit, and right
  now
he can't recall one comforting word from the Bible to save his life.

*****

He might have been able, one day, to pardon Orson Welles
for upsetting the delicate balance of a largely abstracted country,
but he could never forgive the finally undeniable fact that Welles
was only blowing smoke, making up the Martians as he went along.
And my father took personally anything that came through his 1938
state-of-the-art Zenith *Wave-Magnet*. He wanted so much
for just a small part of it to be real, the thrill of a little something
exotic going down in his lifetime, and he'd be there, in the thick of it
for once. He wanted an occasion he could rise to, anything
he could come out on the other side of, better off. And when that
  didn't
truly happen, he took it personally again. Not that he'd really wished
for the end of humanity but, if nothing else, how about
an actual Martian or two he could maybe lift a glass with on the porch,
raising himself—for one colorful night at least—out of the static,
the poor reception his heart's been getting lately.

And so he refused to go to any movie
that Orson Welles went on to make: no *Citizen Kane*, no *Journey
into Fear*. No *Touch of Evil* or *The Lady from Shanghai*. And when he
  heard
that a young hotshot Welles had scripted a few of the President's chats,
he had to turn his back on FDR. He turned off *I Love Lucy* in 1956
when Welles showed up as celebrity guest. And forget about the
  Hallmark
Hall of Fame's *The Man Who Came to Dinner*—not at my father's house.
Later, when Welles' star had fallen so low that he took the role
of TV pitchman for Paul Masson wines, my father would point at him
and say *Orson Welles, you are still an unbelievable horse's ass*
but, really, anyone could see he was still Orson Welles. And my father
was still my father, to that day not so much angry
as incredibly disappointed—as if the Martians, in staying so far away,
were giving him, and him alone, their entire planet's cold, red shoulder.

*****

He saved the daily newspapers that came out in the wake of the

72

broadcast.
He revelled in the way they were going after Welles with a vengeance,
never once acknowledging the self-righteousness of their crusade.
The newsbreaking power of stories in print had been preempted in a
flash
by the electric immediacy of radio, and now the papers were only too
glad
to expose "the perilous irresponsibilities" of the new
and instantly threatening medium: *FCC TO INVESTIGATE RADIO
DRAMA:*
*FAKE RADIO 'WAR' STIRS TERROR THROUGHOUT UNITED
STATES.*

My father lifted them, yellowed and chipping, out of a box in his closet
as if handling unimpeachable state's evidence in the unending trial
of his century. And what he pulled out next astonished me:
a worn record album—"Never Before Released! Not a Single
Dramatic Word Cut! The Most Thrilling Drama Ever Broadcast on
Radio!!!"
He handed it over so unassumingly on an otherwise unremarkable
Sunday
nearly thirty years after the terrible fact of his disenchantment.
You can have it, he told me, and I thought maybe he was finally ready
to let it all go for good.

                    The war in Vietnam was heating up. LBJ
was sweating it out again on the living room television, but I hunkered
down
next to the plastic record player in my upstairs bunker. I would try
to take myself back through my father's life to that night
his nutty and heroic grudge against Orson Welles began.
I set down the needle, closed my eyes, and prepared to become one at
last
with a younger, more excitable, less complicated version of my father.

What I was hearing undeniably had its virtues, technically speaking,
but spinning around that far removed from its greater historical context,
it seemed slightly ridiculous to me—so many unsuspecting people
coming apart, no matter how short-lived their undoing. And secretly
I doubted it was anything I would have fallen for, ever.

                    *****

The lawsuits brought against CBS, the Mercury Theatre and, yes,

against Orson Welles himself, amounted to over a million 1938 dollars
for broken legs, bent fenders, miscarriages, lost wages, and untold
psychic damage. With no obvious precedent on the books
for determining genuine liability, none was ever amply substantiated.
But against the advice of company lawyers, one claim was actually
    settled—
a handwritten note that said:

> *I thought the best thing to do was go away. So I took $3.25 out of my*
> *savings and bought a ticket. After I'd gone sixty miles, I knew it was a play.*
> *Now I don't have money left for the shoes I was saving up for. Would you*
> *please have someone send me a pair of black shoes, size 9-B!*

And Orson Welles himself sent them out in the next day's mail.

       *****

For years, the beleagured citizens in the vicinity of Grovers Mill
preferred not to talk about 1938. Some were vaguely embarrassed,
and the rest were more than fed up with the lingering
sociological attention. But with the fiftieth anniversary looming,
things changed dramatically. The sons and daughters of the sick-and-
    tired
formed a War of the Worlds Committee. They staged a four-day
    celebration
featuring lectures by authentic Princeton astronomers this time,
a Martian costume contest, a dinner dance under the cool October sky
where a local high school band knocked out the ever-popular *Stardust*
before taking its best shot at *Flying Purple People Eater*.
Howard Koch was guest of honor at a full-blown reading of his radio
    script,
although the last half-century had caught up with him, and he begged
    off
taking part in the subsequent Martian Panic 10K Run.
People came unabashedly to embrace their unique station in cultural
    history:
one of the only places on Earth at least a little famous
for what never really happened there.

                   And if my father had been still alive
in 1988, this really might have killed him. No one could have paid him
    enough
to show up, although I don't think the War of the Worlds Committee
    ever

would have given him their serious consideration. They'd been hoping
     for
Orson Welles, who surely would have come if they'd offered him
     enough,
and if he hadn't been three years dead himself. Instead, they issued
a spirited proclamation naming Welles an honorary city father. And
     since I
was the only one of the three of us still alive, it must have been me
saying out loud over morning coffee, over the further droning of the
     radio,
that figures—in honor of my father, that distinctly un-Orson Welles, even
anti-Orson Welles, who was still my only father. I was hoping that—
because I'd finally spoken up, for once taken his side in the eternal
     struggle
against his nemesis—maybe now he'd actually stop talking in my sleep.

                              *****

The last time I was in New Jersey, I drove through Grovers Mill.
I saw the monstrous water tower standing tall on rusted metal legs,
still pockmarked from that night in 1938
when local farmers armed with shotguns roamed the countryside
in the unfathomable dark, looking for no-account Martians to bring
     down.
I found a modest marker: *Historic Site of the Martian Invasion*,
erected by the civic-minded War of the Worlds Committee, who
     apparently
didn't believe that *Historic Site of My Father's Wishful Thinking*
had quite the resonance they were looking for.

I drove north along the Millstone River, half an hour at most, until
I arrived at the more familiar marker with my father's name and dates.
I stood there for a while, trying to think only of the good that came
from his compelling lifelong feud with Orson Welles, from his solemn
     vow
to never again be taken in so absolutely or to have his spirits lifted
so impossibly high. From that disconcerting night forward,
whatever the latest hard-luck wrinkle in his life or anyone else's,
he'd get this nearly wistful look on his face right before conveying
his hard-won assurance—the expression he came to be locally famous
     for:
It's not the end of the world. I was only a little surprised
that it hadn't shown up on his headstone—one last time, for the ages.

                              75

I remember him breaking the news to me when I discovered one of his heroes
for myself: no matter how often the story gets told, in fact there's nothing
even remotely like *I'd rather be in Philadelphia* at the grave of W.C. Fields—
my father's comedy god and frequent Sunday night guest blowhard adversary
of Charlie McCarthy, America's favorite dummy. Millions of listeners
could cite chapter and verse, every sidesplitting putdown
in their celebrated feud.

                   It's not the end of the world, he said, noting
my obvious disappointment. But what good were any of the words we lived by
if it turns out they were never really carved in stone?

In his heart there seemed to be nothing he hadn't heard before—
he'd been to the end of the world as he knew it, and he'd spend
the rest of his life trying to make it mostly back, carrying with him
the dead weight of that astonishing Martian no-show. I wanted to say
at last I understood why he could never let it go. But I didn't.
I still couldn't imagine walking those last forty years in his shoes.
Maybe Orson Welles would have tried to do right by my father, too,
if he'd had even an inkling of this egregious and longstanding wrong—
and then if only he'd known exactly what kind of apology
my father might have been persuaded, finally, to try on for size.

               *****

The same man who never found it in himself to forgive Orson Welles
always managed to forgive me so completely, it was frightening.
Every one of my effortless childhood transgressions, promises like so many
broken windows, the bad-necktie gifts I repeatedly signed off on,
the dents I put in his beloved Chevrolet on the Edison Diner parking lot,
where it was invariably half-past bar-time: *It's not the end of the world.*
Even when I couldn't stop myself from watching—in the sanctity
of his own living room, on his first-ever color TV—George Pal's 1953
War of the Worlds five nights in a row on *Million Dollar Movie*
(this time the Martians arrived in California, buzzed around in genuine
flying saucers, and were subsequently A-bombed, and Orson Welles
had nothing to do with that): *It's not the end of the world.*
This was his generous absolution, and more—his grudging lifetime

guarantee that even when things fell short of the best anyone could
    hope for,
believe him, they could always be worse, no matter how unthinkable
    that was
as I pondered the inscrutable arithmetic of high school. Add to that
the goggle-eyed mysteries of shop class. Take away Debbie Fuller, lost
to her family's inexcusable decision to leave town.
                            Whatever happened
to that moony girl you were sweet on? and I wasn't about to say
Princeton, because without a doubt that would have got him going, and
for nothing. For all I saw of her again, it might as well have been Mars.

        *****

Here is where, at last, it has to end—where enough will finally
be enough: this oddball song of abiding love for someone who became
convinced he was a different man after 1938. And his unrequited feud
with the person he so tenaciously held responsible. This is the end
all good things must come to, for better or for worse.
                          So take this,
Orson Welles: in the name of the father and the son who survived him,
you are here forgiven. And Howard Koch, who gave back the world
in *Casablanca,* four quick years after masterminding its destruction:
forgiven. For FDR, a newer, better deal on his place in history than the
    one
he ultimately got from my father. This is for the Martians, who fell
short of my father's expectations, who chose to stay home, wanting
    nothing
really to do with humankind. For the small towns scarcely on anyone's
    map
and the people who think they can leave them behind on their frantic
    way
to somewhere else. For Debbie Fuller: I have to admit that it wasn't
the end of the world. This is for the ghostly world of all our fathers,
so far now beyond the pale that they can't be bothered anymore—

but especially for my father, younger than I ever knew him, before
the Great Disheartening: the Sunday comics pages are still unfolded
on the kitchen table. In the kaleidoscopic desert of Coconino County,
Krazy Kat gets beaned on the noggin by another sure-fire Ignatz brick
and keeps on singing just the same, strangely more in love than ever.
And Buck Rogers is cruising his colorful 25th Century, coming to the
    last-
minute rescue in his super-autogyrospectomoscope. But that's 500

years away.
And my father's still sitting close to his spiffy, dependable Zenith,
still laughing at Bergen and McCarthy until it hurts, because
there's so much going on already in the world that's nothing to laugh
    at—
and he's not about to change the station this time.

SCOTT COFFEL

Cockeyed Louie

In the welfare state of heaven the pamphlets promise
that even cockeyed Louie with his glum Chihuahua,
with the lewd postcard in his pocket
and the Hebrew god on his tongue, with his forty years of
    drudgery
and his cramped apartment next to the incinerator chute
and his trips to the Food Fair taking hours for a bag
of peppers and light bulbs and toilet paper and dog food,
that even he shall know an end

to the injustice and the carnage
and the boredom: cockeyed Louie, who blessed
the sanctity of unions on summer nights under the vapor-lamps,
cursing the rich while his irritated dog squeaked at mosquitoes:
cockeyed Louie,
who wept for my father at the synagogue, who kept his distance
after Labor Day, whose clothes grew fearfully loose by
    November,
who by April had disappeared entirely.

CAROLE COHEN

Thanksgiving Day Prayer

I give thanks this day for commodities
that allow me to gamble on my nation's
food supply and eat well from my winnings.
I give thanks, O Lord, for knowing the value
of hard work and how money flows
to those deserving, how investment capital
reflects Thy blessings and bounty.

I am thankful my skin is not black, the color
of sin, and I am thankful most blacks
know their place most of the time.
I am thankful I am not lazy, leaning
on the shoulder of welfare, crying
piteously in the dark for a handout.
You help us who help ourselves.

And thank you, Lord, that I was not born
female, carry my genitals outside
my skin for all to admire, not hide
my sex within and use it like a secret
only a few can know. My masculinity
commands and protects the weaker sex,
enables them to populate, to serve our will.

Thank you for the spacious lands
that provide oil, streams that carry off
our waste and this whole huge earth
on which we reap so many species of animals.
This is truly a garden, and I thank you for it.
Thank you for our laws which protect us
from the bastards who try to exist

(no stanza break)

80

outside the garden, who break down
our gates and will not work for us
in the way we want.

I thank you for my good judgment,
for politics that discipline and weaken
our enemies here and abroad, for The Party
which protects me and gives me tax breaks
at the expense of those who would take advantage
of my wealth. Thank you
for our soldiers who mete your justice
to the world and stamp out religions
that are pagan and sinful, governments
that don't agree with our good way of life.
How good to know for sure what is wrong,
to be born certain I am right. In your name
I pray: *Thank you, Lord.*
Amen.

ROBERT CORDING

Inspiration—

The name he gave an ordinary Sears lawn chair
To which he attached forty-two weather balloons,
Each seven feet in diameter and, with the sun
And early commuter traffic, took off from
His own backyard, a small patch of ground
No larger than ten by thirty yards, and rose
Sixteen thousand feet, his impossibly possible
Comic ascension witnessed by a five year old girl
Who would not stop waving from her Long Beach
Front yard, his girl friend, and a pilot, TWA 231,
Who calmly radioed, *we have a man in a lawn chair*
Suspended from balloons in our ten o'clock position.

"I thought about it all through Vietnam, thought
It had to be possible, must be possible," he told
The police when he finally came down, higher than
He'd ever been, though his flight ended sooner
Than he expected and not as he planned, his deflated
Balloons tangled in electric lines of a suburb
Ten miles away. He never made the Mojave of
His destination, and he never crossed over
The San Gabriels, but once up above the rooftops,
He found the perspective he was looking for,
And watched the fast disappearing street corners,
And the highways repeating Wal-Mart, K-Mart,
Burger King, McDonalds, Taco Bell give way

To the Queen Mary and the crazy seaplane
Of Howard Hughes and, higher up, Catalina Island
Floated like an earthly cloud in the blue sky
Of the Pacific. The sky kept getting bigger,

(no stanza break)

82

The clouds spoke in a language all their own
At ten thousand feet and, in the clear cold air,
He began to see the face of the girl he'd left
in Viet Nam, the most lovely girl he'd ever known.
In the distance, the San Gabriels lay neatly folded.
At sixteen thousand feet, his toes beginning
To freeze, it seemed a man could purify his spirit.

So why not leave him there in his lawn chair,
Waving to the TWA pilot, the naked kingdoms
Of the human heart rising in the sky? Why
Bring him down, attach this epilogue:
In time he lost his girlfriend, read nothing
But the Bible, pitched his tent higher
And higher in the mountains until one night,
His shoes placed neatly at the tent's opening,
He climbed into his sleeping bag, put a pistol
To his chest and shot himself in the heart.

ANN CROSSMAN

Fanfare to the Common Man
For the men and women serving in the 134th battalion

BDUs are overrated.
What are we buckin hiding from
on post? Everyone knows
we're here, surrounded by concrete and loud trucks
the color of trees,
You think I'm gonna blend in?

I went to witty blast normal school
for three hours a day in a booth
facing the wall. Dan—she hit
me with that ruler
like some passed over beauty queen, and then
I went to the voc joke
to work on cars.
It, I don't need that.

My mama said I was nothing
and it was drugs or war
for me. She made me join
the drab army. Yuck, either way
it's prison. It's not like I got a resume
or somein.

The army's all about bitty jobs
that don't mean nothing. We
clean the streets every week even tho
patrol don't go that far. Sarge
say, if it don't grow, it go.
Muck, if we're in luck, the gut truck
will roll by—better than the mess
on post.

I got one girl telling me she's pregnant
but she witchen lied to me. My boy
is two back home and if
his mama sticks around
while I'm gone, I might marry her
when I get back. My mama's takin care of him
and keeps itchen me about keeping my thing
in my pants.

I need to pass this ban test
to get outta here and get a better
assignment. Odd man, if one of them
tries to pull anything on me, I'll
grab my gun and nail em. We're
getting our masses beat
just for riding the train home.
I don't care who we're protectin,
puck, I'm here to protect me.

CARL DENNIS

Fire

Though I don't begrudge the fighters of wild fires
The praise they receive in the papers,
Wedged in among stories of scandals and wars,
I think I deserve some mention myself
For damping down, last night in the restaurant,
The fire of my resentment.
It wasn't easy to find my declaration of joy
At being the friend of the woman I dined with
Interrupted by an old acquaintance of hers
Who fixed himself by her chair for twenty minutes
While he filled her in on his recent triumphs.

If I couldn't douse my anger, didn't I try at least
Not to fan the flames but to climb above them
To the lofty look out where it's easy to see
How blessed I am for a friend whose concern
Isn't confined to the few in her inner circle.
Didn't I tell myself she wouldn't have looked
So beautiful if she'd spoken a few cold words
To a self-important intruder and turned back to me.

True, a sign that the fire still reaches me
Came after he left, when I didn't welcome her back
As she deserved, as if returning at last
After years of working abroad in famine relief
And building schools, without a penny in payment.
But wouldn't the words I blurted, in a tone of remonstrance,
"Your dinner's cold," make it easier for readers
To interpret any praise I receive in the papers
As available to people like them, not to heroes only?

What about you? Do you stand by the story
You've told since high school, how once,
Walking home after the New Year's dance with a girl
Whose voice you still haven't forgotten,
You didn't flame up when a car full of her friends
Passed without slowing down to offer a ride,
Friends who never included you in their circle,
How you shrugged off the snub to spare her feelings?

Isn't it time to move beyond vanity
And acknowledge what really happened,
How they stopped to offer a ride to her,
How she, who had farther to walk in the cold
Than you, politely declined? Isn't it time to admit
How sweet that gift was, how it made
A winter night feel suddenly summery,
With a gentle summer rain wetting the undergrowth
To make a wild fire improbable.

See, you're a lucky man, just as I am,
Saved from the flames by miraculous intervention.
And now you might try asking yourself,
If you haven't already, what needs to be done
To wrap a gift like that one and pass it on.

We are pleased to announce results for
The Marjorie J. Wilson Award
for 2003

FIRST PRIZE: $2,500 & Publication
(Contest Judge: ROBERT PINSKY)
is awarded to:

"Outside the Mainway Market"
by:
CATHERINE DOTY
of Saint Paul, Minnesota

FINALISTS

CAROLINE HEMPHILL, Chicago, IL
TRAPETA B. MASON, Philadelphia, PA
SUSANNA MISHLER, Anchorage, AK
JOHN T. MUIR, Ireland
BARBARA PAPARAZZO, Conway, MA
YOSEFA RAZ, Berkeley, CA
SUZANNE RICHARDSON, Havre, MT
PETRA UHRIG, Saratoga Springs, NY
CATHERINE WING, Seattle, WA

CATHERINE DOTY

Outside the Mainway Market

"Every day," our mother says,
"kids die on those goddamned things"
and she nods at the lone yellow horse
with the red vinyl bridle
and four black, shining hooves
like police hat brims.
Not only do we stop our five-part
begging, we walk wide around the beast,
though Mary brushes the coin box
with her sleeve.

Rigid in flight, the great horse's legs
flange out toward us. Not one of us argues.
We hold onto our mother's coat, cross
several streets, touch the dog we always touch
when we walk home, fingering
his freckled snout. Then we scream
and run in the yard while supper cooks,
and the sky shudders pale for some seconds
before it darkens, as if in that lavender moment,
three blocks away, a child drops
the reins and gasps as his shoes fly off,
and plumes of smoke rise
from the crown of his hand-knit hat.

CATHERINE DOTY

Mrs. Vooren's Calendar

Each time her son would crap
she'd write it down: EBM
for Ellsworth, Bowel Movement,
though she was a cockney
and called it "moving your barrels,"
which put me in mind
of dragging the trash cans in
a moment before Zito's bread truck
sent them spinning. Once, at our house,
Mrs. Vooren and my mom talking,
Ellsworth tore out of our bathroom,
yelped out "yes!", and Mrs. V.
popped up like a prairie dog,
grabbed a black crayon, and scrawled
EBM on my mom's new calendar,
three tarry letters as thick as clusters
of flies, under smiling Miss Rheingold
ablaze in snowy skiwear. Our mother
preferred not to know what came out
of us, and when once I managed
to go in the Vooren's bathroom,
where a fifty-pound net bag of onions
slumped next to the tub, I told her
I'd gone, and she just snapped,
"You flushed, yes, m'duck?" and shoved
me outside to read comic books with Ellsworth,
that cosseted turnip, that prig, that mama's boy,
that temple of virtue, that little sack of shit.

DENISE DUHAMEL

I've Been Known

to spread it on thick to shoot off my mouth to get it off my chest
    to tell him where
    to get off
to stay put to face the music to cut a shine to go under to sell
    myself short to play
    myself down
to paint the town to fork over to shell out to shoot up to pull a
    fast one to go haywire
    to take a shine to
to be stuck on to glam it up to vamp it up to get her one better to
    eat a little higher
    on the hog
to win out to get away with to go to the spot to make a stake to
    make a stand to
    stand for something to stand up for
to snow under to slip up to go for it to take a stab at it to try out
    to go places to play
    up to get back at
to size up to stand off to slop over to be solid with to lose my
    shirt to get myself off
    to get myself off the hook

RUSSELL EDSON

The Civilized Man

      When going out he would wear handcuffs in case he committed
a crime; a
good citizen ready to be arrested. Okay, officer, you've got me dead to
rights. Perhaps
you'll want to give me a good whack on my head with your nightstick?
Well, go
ahead, until proven innocent I shall remain guilty, leaving it in your
hands to find
my innocence.
      Perhaps I shall be proven criminally insane. Then I shall
demand a
straightjacket as my democratic right, and take up residence in a room
made of rubber.
Sometimes this is the only decent thing left to a civilized man...

DAN ENCARNACION

One Aspect of Appreciating a Fine Cigar is the Pleasure Derived from Rotating the Smooth, Tight, Cylindrical Shaft Slowly Between the Thumb and Coupled First and Second Fingers, Then Feeling for Firmness

The high school jocks roll unconscious Zuni.
They cut off their fourth fingers as a tal-
Isman of mettle or, perhaps, terminal ennui.

It happens every Welfare Check Day—a spree
Of drunken rigor to spirit away their dismissal.
The high school jocks roll unconscious Zuni.

The jocks confiscate the government money.
The jocks must think their raids done most noble.
Is man of mettle or, perhaps, terminal ennui?

The jocks sever the superfluous pinky.
They allow a Zuni to keep his opposable thumb.
The high school jocks roll unconscious Zuni.

Three fingers and a thumb can still grasp a bottle of beer.
The jocks grasp the notion of cyclical time.
Is man of mettle or, perhaps, terminal ennui?

The high school jocks watch the phases of the week.
They know when it is a good day to get drunk.
The high school jocks roll unconscious Zuni.
Is man of mettle or, perhaps, terminal ennui?

DAN ENCARNACION

Grammar

She will die.
My mother.
She will die. She has died. She died. She dies. She is dying. She
    is dead.

I will die.
My self.
I will die. I have died. I died. I die. I am dead.

(many deaths
      for a person to live).

In the hospital, my mother was panicking.
This was before she accepted her death. This was the first time
    she was to die.
The first time we were told she could die at any moment, at any
    second.
My mother didn't want me to leave her bedside.
My sister said, if that should happen, just leave; she won't notice
    you're gone.
My sister is a nurse. My sister has been a nurse. My sister nurses.
                                     My sister nursed.

When I was born, my mother had breast cancer.
She had one breast. The other had been removed.
I did not nurse. I will not nurse. I have not nursed. I do not
    nurse.

My mother told me that I gave her hemorrhoids when I was
    born.
I gave my mother hemorrhoids. I have given my mother

(no stanza break)

94

hemorrhoids. I had
  given my mother hemorrhoids. I give my mother
hemorrhoids. I am
      giving my mother hemorrhoids.

In the hospital, my mother was panicking. She groped for me.
Her paper gown flew open as she grabbed my arm as I stepped
    away.
She was crying and screaming hysterically. Take me away.
I saw my mother's pubis. The first time. First time since my
    birth, that is.
I was too young to remember the real first time. My eyes were
    still shut.
I have seen my mother's pubis. I saw my mother's pubis. I will
    see my mother's
                        pubis. I am my mother's pubis.

Walk away because you can.
The only person who will know is you.
You know. You have known. You will know. You are knowing.

A person should not be allowed to see his mother's pubis when
    she can die at
                    any moment, naked, in front of that person's eyes.
A person should not be allowed to see his mother's pubis when
    she is hysterical
                    with the labor of death.

She labored. She labors.

RHINA P. ESPAILLAT

Shelter

How clever of my neighbor to devise
this little cage of nets in his front yard
to keep his children—and the toys they guard—
safe in the larger cage of Papa's eyes.

He's strung it between trees, by curtain hooks
from which four airy walls hang down: inside,
a wooden pony small enough to ride,
if you are small enough to read cloth books.

Light rain has grizzled the straw mane, and lends
weight to the text of flowery ABC's;
today rider and reader, on their knees,
are coloring indoors with noisy friends.

All of this bounded by the flimsiest fence;
its maker knows the stranger passing through
armed with a knife would know just what to do
to make a mockery of confidence.

And still my clever neighbor girds about
his irreplaceable—his priceless—things,
as if he knew some charm in sticks or strings
to keep the treasure in, the danger out.

SUSAN FAIRFIELD

Evensong

You won't find Zen persimmons in this poem,
or Zion. Each line I write might be a
stun-gun. Or a Sahara (a khamsin,
a simoom) or a spermy squirt of amber-

gris in a whorish sea. Each word,
shoved on an ice floe like an Inuit elder,
drifts toward...what? A lambent myth,
phantasm of deliverance? Or a bear's

sudden teeth? Dear heart, don't be afraid.
Remember how we spent an August nightfall
watching the soft ping ping of lights flick
onto the mauve, then onto the black, until

the sky was starshot. How I lay on the grass
weeping, unable to rise. Speechless.

MELANIE FIGG

Soul's Road

1. Houses of Beauty

The breeze from the river   passes over us
drying in tents   on the west bank of the Nile.

Salts & resins & desert wind—
      what can happen if you give it long enough?

Waiting for time to make   it's mark on you

              to matter
              to make of the body a reckoning

This is how we too often lived our lives—the sheltered heart

       hungry but wary & retreating before time.

It has not made it easier, this preservation, it has not made it
   more familiar—

          we wait & our bodies become

     a map we have never imagined, our skin beautiful &

holding the afternoon light,

                the cotton sheets not quite
  wings—

2. Canopic Jars

For the lungs, a baboon head—
For the liver, a human—
For the intestines, a falcon—
The stomach, a jackal. Wild dogs
keep me up at night, worrying if
you meant what you said, if what
I said fell too hard. Is this what eternity feels like?

The weight of the word bearing down—

                     & this fever, this stubborn need

to make this body yours, this vessel I will put

      in your hands regardless—

           take, eat—this has always been yours—

3. Gazelle-Headed Guardian Demon

This animal—her cornered rage, her bottomless storm—nothing

           gets by her version of things. She'll keep

                the world away if
anything can—

her wit can shipwreck. Her eyes are bruised, endlessly
   discerning—

       There is nothing that is unafraid.
       She howls into the space she has cleared:

you can't have her yet—

unrequited, she sneers & spooks. Her success

leaves her anxious: peace cannot come to this body, cannot even
be imagined—

& death takes what it will.

4. Opening of the Mouth

Tilt the head back until   the throat is a bridge

                              where words are painted
across this world's lining.

                    I am the way in & back & through & they use their
fingers,

the priests, they take a wooden tool & pry open my lips:

            the mouth revives & carries
                              the truth   becomes a
residence

to welcome back the soul / this song still moving in me—

                    like how a lover cleaves & makes of this body
reconciled land

            from which to unfold & take flight

5. Book of the Dead

too often paradise is what you don't have   what you can't
imagine yours

100

in ancient Egypt paradise was a world of canals & lush forests

                      paradise is a cleaving

is where you are waiting, the echo that calls to reckon—to pass
    through & be reborn:

I have made none to weep.
I have not robbed the poor.
        Truth feathers and tattoos my tongue—
I have learned to be content with what is mine.

                        What I speak will last and re-make
        this world

                                        as a bird lost in song
        I will sing—

SUSAN FIRER

The Star Club Portal

Some three-quarters hour after
her last earth breath, long
after she was declared dead,
I changed her clothes. I
enlisted her nurse to help
hold her body in
a sitting position. It was
as if we were playing
together on a summer porch, but
we were together in the hospice's
dim lit room. I took
the string ties of her
washed-thin-flower-sprigged hospital
gown and undid them,
as if they were all that was
between us, and in the candle
of the blue single iris I brought, I
took the gown off the top half of her.
There were the large breasts
I knew so well! Welcome! Welcome!
her mole, the red triangle of skin
where her blouses never
buttoned. I folded
the hospital gown down over
the bottom half of her body.

MAXWELL FOX

Is

She was bridge she was
                  Where the river ran
                            As sludge
                  She smacked

Her rudder
              In and out the wheelie water
                      Dee la dee la died dahd

All through
                  A lot of brothers'
                Fudge.

Minnie Moonie
        I'm from Miss
            Our
            I

                      My mammy
              Jesus Loves
Where she come from.

ALICE FRIMAN

Eyesore

To the west, Blacks.
To the east and southeast down the bend,
Whites. Between, the old couple—Monacan Indian,
perhaps the last—grazing their skinny cows,
hoeing their patch. The Mister once said, sure
he remembered me, but how *could* he, me coming
maybe five times in twenty years. But for me
he was fixture, made to order—baggy overalls,
grizzled cheek working a wad, Chevy pickup
up on blocks. One rusted geranium.

Now six years later I return—
country road, meadows, the old poplar
shimmying down one more October. My movie,
my pastoral, just waiting for me to walk my walk
and take my place. What didn't hold tight
until I came back? Even that brown dog
trembling like a lover, showed up each day
to bark his heart out to my empty spot.

*   *   *

There are two kinds of not seeing—
when you can't or when you don't.
If you suffer from the latter, better depend
on shock, immense fallacies, mackerel
falling from the skies or in this case
an empty yellow school bus careening hell-
bent around the bend headed for disaster or,
like a ghost on fire, fleeing one. A patch
spliced from a grade B movie to fill the hole
big as a bus left by what was missing.

The old man, gone—truck, barn,
house, the works. I tramp the empty yard,
trying to conjure up the groaning porch,
the ripped screen door, the annual geranium
anemic in its pot. But light glares.
The movie has let out early. And look.
Nothing but neatness and hush in a plot too flat
for these Virginia hills, and tread marks
running back and forth like a crazed eraser
with purple wildflowers scrambling over it fast
as if they knew what's buried there and would tell you
if they could take the time to stop.

PATRICIA L. FRISELLA

To the Ignorant Countries Where Civilians Die Insufficiently

I came then to the towers of Babylon in Chicago
which had stood the tests of time and invasion.
Wind howled through hollowed tunnels like tornadoes,
lifting sewer lids, tormenting the homeless.
It moaned over hallowed cables with monocles
and knuckled fists raised in the language of vengeance.

Each generation has wars called progress,
has wastelands called victory, has dead
heroes; they fall like dominoes to the ground
where they lay face to face with the dying and the dead.

The roads of Duone, Atholl and Drummond Rise
lead to Dunblane. All roads lead to Columbine,
Kosovo or Palestine. I am the stubborn last ember
of a smoldering passion, the nearly dead reaching out
the pleading hand, the weak begging the helpless for aid;

there's enough to do taking care of this business of living
in unheated tenements among starving silverfish
and angry rats; my message is squashed, squandered,
red, but not for long; I am knocked down, toed

like road-kill to the gutter. What remains of life
flows seaward. You know what I was; you see that I've become
a hugger of phone poles. I tell them my secret – the doorknobs
are marching tonight. I cannot bathe in the water; soiled
tampons, alligators, kitchen grease and poison scare me.

Is this cabalism or malady? The tentacles of Rome

(no stanza break)

106

grope across time with confusing capitals; I'm lost
in the imagined millennium with new stadiums
for gladiators stuttering backward with names
like Regurgitation and Flagellation;

I am an alien. You are not my people.
I do not worship at your altar. I have studied
the tilled earth of many short lives, turning up charred bones
and land-mines, all the hidden markers
that lead to the rope, the blade, the gun.

I smell the starch and hot irons
of lingering Puritans, still scowling
with puttied faces and dreary minds;
I shed light on their lies and they scatter
like roaches to the dark corners of their belief
in thou shalt not and the second amendment;
my shades shutter upward to let in belugas,
bluebirds and bumblebees.

I have lived so long in the fluorescent air
of the imminent bomb, the atomic beheading,
I can ignore its daily buzz,
planes and trucks and fast cars,
easy spending, repeat,
forget and repeat.

A doctor flying blind with an ice pick
fifty years ago might have lanced my skull,
the lobotomy leaving me to loll
away my life. Now, I wander the streets
in sloshing galoshes, drooling and muttering.
It has always been hard to be good
or we would not still need a savior.

FRANK GIAMPIETRO

Hearing This Kind of Thing

Food meant nothing to Glen Gould, he could go for hours
without thinking of it. Because of this, I suppose
I should like his music, but I just feel jealous.
I myself never engage
in anything food doesn't make better.
In fact, most of the time, I prefer just the food.

Wallace Stevens looks as though he was well-fed.
He was the vice-president of an insurance company.
He said, poetry is "the desire to contain
the world within one's perception of it." I'm at this moment
reminded of my wife who made this most excellent
fudge and how she brought it to me with a cup of coffee
on a tray saying, chocolate dreams of coffee and it
dreams of chocolate. Surely she has contained the world
by making it, and if not by making it, then by thinking
to bring me a piece of it with coffee on a tray. She never
writes down the ingredients for whatever it is
she's cooking; she claims making food like this helps her
not eat it. And she just loves Glen Gould.

Did I mention her incredible skills of comprehension?
I've known her to recite the entire plots of movies, scene
by scene. I heard Sonny Rollins
could do the same thing with melodies, that often he wouldn't
even need to hear the end to know how it ends. But

that was a minor jealousy, and anyway, I mean I don't know,
but doesn't a melody always end on the note it started with?

FRANK GIAMPIETRO

On Not Actually Having Been Born on the Moon

Denise Duhamel writes a lot like me. I name her
because another poet said I should, said it would be "disingenuous" not
to.
Isn't that a great word. Reminds me of this old & very famous poet
whose name I don't recall who rhymed hippopotamus with
monotonous.
I told my Dad today that it was his generation who ruined poetry
for the public. I probably should have said I write
a lot like Denise Duhamel but I don't think she would mind.
Her husband is a pretty big guy.
He's also a poet. My wife is not. She's into pottery. Don't think
I haven't noticed how close the spelling is to poetry though.
My old friend Jean who has his Ph.D. now, who calls
every once in a while to tell me about his latest rare art purchase
asked if we have a lot of ashtrays lying around the house.
He's actually a very nice guy. Denise Duhamel is also very nice.
So is her husband.
The now famous writer Jonathan Franzen was married to a writer.
When they were first married they did nothing but write all morning
and read all afternoon. They split when he started to publish.
He said as much as he hated to admit it, jealousy was a factor.
The poet who told me to name Denise Duhamel, whose name
is Julianna Baggott, can't stand Franzen.
Julianna won't allow his name to be spoken in her house.
Julianna has three small and beautiful children.
I often imagine them lying around the house. She calls Franzen the "F"
word.
She has published a book of poems and 2 novels. I'm always
encouraging
my wife to show her pottery.

Last night my wife and I took our 2 year old son to this giant furniture
store

(no stanza break)

109

to look at king-size beds. The sales lady wasn't surprised how he went
  crazy leaping
from sofa to bed to armoire to coffee table. She says it's something
  about furniture stores
and children his age. Anyway we were there to get a king-size bed—
Another suggestion from my friend Julianna Baggott, the poet and
  novelist.
She said for her last kid they didn't even put up the crib.
I think my mom secretly thinks we made a big mistake by getting our
  son
in the habit of sleeping with us. I say us but until we get the king-size
  bed, them.
I sleep on the couch. The last time I tried to sleep with them I sang
  songs
to my son all night in my dreams. My son is in music school and also
  tiny tumblers.
Denise Duhamel doesn't have any kids
right now as far as I know. She said when we met she'd be happy to
stay in touch. That was three years ago. She has her own website.
I'd tell you what it is but I tried to find it last night and couldn't.
Maybe I need a new search engine.
She has this great poem about winning a grant for poetry and blowing it
  on a trip to
France and while there going to a nude beach and feeling at first
  incredibly self
conscious. Gee I hope she won't mind that I said all that.
This is not how this poem began.
The first draft was way too chatty. I'm not even sure I'm going to keep
the same title now. I'm reading a lot of Hart Crane. I love his short
  lyric
poems. But don't be too impressed, I claim to like him when I can't
  even claim to have
read "The Bridge."
In fact that's what I'm supposed to be doing right now instead of this
--according to me of course. So who's Hart Crane? Exactly, my father
would say. My father grew up in New York City, too. I like to think
  that maybe his
mother's apartment was one that my dad delivered ice to.
Anyway, the poem I had written with the same title as this poem
went on and on about an old idea I had for a poem
about how I wasn't actually born on the moon
but was instead born on the day of the moon landing July 20, 1969.

(no stanza break)

110

And how that somehow made me special
when you consider how Moses was set adrift in a river
and Jesus was born in a manger. To tell the truth
I'd be tickled pink just to publish a book of poems.
So one of the books I got on Hart Crane goes on
and on about his total lack of irony. I thought about
naming my next child Hart if it's a boy
but Hart doesn't go well with Giampietro.
We're hoping for a girl anyway. I keep trying to write about things
other than myself but it always comes back to this. Marvin Bell hates
    my poems.
Hate is too strong a word. Don't ask me how I know. At the furniture
    store,

I couldn't keep my son away from these balls they had lying around.
They were everywhere and in every shape and size.
There was this big heavy one near the Hemmingway "Amazon
    Collection."
My son just loves balls. The point is they weren't actually balls,
they were just decoration. Which reminds me of how
the ER doctor who lives across the street asked me once if I was
    worried
people would steal my poems when I sent them out
and didn't understand when I said no because they're not worth that
    much.
It reminds me of that because we really want to buy a nice bed,
one that we can pass down to our children someday. And the nice ones,
the ones with no veneer turn out to be incredibly expensive.
The balls on the other hand, even the Hemmingway ball,
as beautiful and substantial as it was, was only 5 bucks.
This poem originally went on and on about how Denise Duhamel wrote
    these terrific
couple of poems about the moon.
To be honest reading them made me jealous as hell.
I recommend them.
I'm going to ask my poet novelist friend Julianna Baggott what she
    thinks of this version.
Then I'm going to ask Denise Duhamel what she thinks of Marvin Bell.

111

ROBERT GIBB

Gregory's Scrapping

Perhaps you've passed him on the Rankin Bridge,
Heading back from the scrap yard in Braddock—
The slow child of the boroughs, retarded at birth.

He's steadily peddling, waving you by, tricycle bin
Emptied of its stash: cans and copper piping, bright
Compacted balls of foil. 7 AM and he's been at work

For an hour now, mists slowly burning off the river
Where great carp lurk, the color of sunken brass.
He'd salvage them too if he could, wring a few bucks

Extra these days when a good haul means aluminum
At thirty cents a pound and a bike that doesn't
Breakdown while freighting it. Scrap's hard to find

Now that Park Corporation has picked things clean.
Dawn-to-dusk shifts he's out there, in whatever kind
Of weather, checking Lapko's and Chiodo's bars,

The lot next to Shop 'n Save. A good day means
That jacket, his name in stitched light flashing from
Its satin on the road to Homestead and Hays,

The sun's braid crowning the horizon, and everywhere
He looks there's metal left out on the ground.
On a good day the leaf of its rust turns to gold.

DEBRA GINGERICH

Gap

At the Rockvale Outlets next to a patchwork quilt of color-
coordinated socks, you cut me off in line to request directions to
a restaurant where you might find some Amish or at least some
Mennonites. You—hoisted up by shopping bags from Mikasa,
Hugo Boss, and Donna Karin—ask the cashier what it's like to
live among them. Do the buggies get in the way? You're in my
way of picking up a quick pair of cheap Gap jeans before I drive
home in my husband's bull of a car. Me, a cheerleader in a short
pleated skirt, voted most energetic of my senior class, who has
never buried my blond, sometimes dyed copper, hair under a
prayer covering. I watch *Star Trek*, own two cell phones, you
ignorant urban schmuck. I drank Chianti and danced to *Blue Moon*
as a tattoo of a dove peaked out the shoulder of my sleeveless
wedding dress. And this is how some Mennonites cut our bangs
short, sassy from an issue of *Celebrities Hairstyle*. I want to offer
you a Pennsylvania Dutch obscenity or something else of the
Mennonite experience you're not looking for—a conversation
about the Reformation, how Jacob Ammon led a schism over
shunning or the impact of reading *Martyr's Mirror* on a child. But
the Amish Farm Museum across the street only offers carriage
rides through the covered bridge until five and the cashier just
finished writing directions to the Good & Plenty Restaurant.
Tonight you'll feast on creamed corn and Shoofly pie while I
microwave my TV dinner into rubbery, stir-fried oblivion.

JAMES STONE GOODMAN

Blessing

Bo Diddley loved me
I dug deep and I sang from my joint
I love you, Bo Diddley said to me,
I love how you dig it
dive deep
always go deep
said Bo Diddley.

Dig the elemental, Bo Diddley said,
what's your name.
Dig the elemental and do the woodshedding
don't be pretty, said Bo Diddley.

Little Richard dug me
Richard and I made the tunes together
we sang them slowly
wound that tempo way down
then we brought it up, high up,
we surprised everybody.
Go deep, Richard said, *dig.*

I dug,
dug so deep
when the bass player didn't thump it
dug so deep
when the drummer didn't show up
dug so deep
when the preacher talked too long
I collapsed.

You hurt yourself

(*no stanza break*)

114

the crawlin' black snake said
you hurt yourself because you went deep
when you go there you go without your skin
into the dark.

Don't go alone if you can help it, said Bo Diddley.
Take me and Richard with you.

DEBORA GREGER

Letter Four Hundred Years Late

Dear WS,
           With goat hair and straw,
they have rebuilt your Globe.
On the south bank of the Thames it squats,
so clean you wouldn't recognize it.
From the New World they come to see
your plays performed your way:
men wearing dresses mince about in corsets.
They speak in the voices of mice.

What was it about, that play of yours?
Was that supposed to be your ghost in the shadows,
forcing its way through a thicket of chairs,
catching the drift of a thimble of thistledown
that fell from the false ceiling, a real sky.
It bumped into a pillar, then into a fool.
The man who played the queen caught your ghost
with her train, dragging you along.
I'm sorry. I cried against my will.

And then, your words were drowned out
as, over that "O" left open to the elements,
a jet from the Orient wormed its way
down the worn path to Heathrow.
How like actors, the shadows taking their time
to fall! When the last dead man had been
applauded off the stage, only you remained.

Some had bought T-shirts bearing your face
like a "Wanted" poster Was it really you?
Fair as a feast day was your blank forehead.
Were you the shade who trailed us downriver
to the Underground? Nothing has changed.

A second Elizabeth sits, a mouse
on a moth-eaten throne, and will not scare.
Her three weak sons she's yet to wean
from the dribbling wet-nurse of the public purse.
Lesser men are softened by cruelty,
whether to sing the truth or a more fragrant lie.

In the Underground, across the tracks, a rat,
dressed for the evening in the finest soot,
made an entrance through the velvet of grime.
A small dark thing with a plague to its name,
it did not flinch or flee as, with a steely scream,
the last train of the night arrived. Oh, that we
could sit again on the river bank and hear
you tell sad stories of the death of kings.

DEBORA GREGER

The Geography of Dream

Bumper to bumper, the nuclear engineers
crawled home from work, but my father
was no longer among them. In retirement,
he sat on his patio, flaking an arrowhead.

My old street, back in the Stone Age!
My soul, I left you there, explaining yourself
to a friendly mosquito. Once a week
a truck drove by, spraying something

that smelled of death on a summer evening.
Boys rode their bikes in its sour-sweet fog,
away from their mothers calling forlornly,
furiously calling. How did I come

to stand on the steps of a church long torn down,
at the feet of my eighth-grade teacher.
Sister Martin Mary wore the old habit,
the one I thought she'd long ago abandoned.

Yards of black serge swathed all but her face,
as if she had no need of a body.
"Why have you come back?" she asked.
"I thought I dismissed you long ago."

Someone I once had been sat on the ugly couch
in my parents' living room, waiting to give
the performance of her life. The front door was open,
cottonwoods murmuring. *Listen*, they said.

Don't listen to us. We're stuck here. Give us a drink.

JOHN GREY

Adventures in Poverty

With each scrape of pen,
I can feel the check I write
suck blood from my bank account.
I open my wallet a little
so the flies won't escape,
so the presidents don't know
they're all Washington.
When I wake up in the morning,
I'm constantly asking myself
do I have the funds for this day,
is the light cheap enough,
can I pay the bill for the clouds
and the sky and the grass, the trees,
and the wind that shakes them.
There's a woman in the bed beside me
but she's like a pawn shop
I take my feelings to.
Sure I say, "I love you,"
but what I really mean is,
"What can I get for this?"
My books are all second hand
but who knows how many hands
have really thumbed through them.
The food in my cupboards
smell of the coupons I bought them with.
Anything of value in my rooms
feels like it's stolen from the guy
who used to have a good-paying job.
The problem is I've got company,
a roof over my head,
clothes to wear, sustenance aplenty,

(*no stanza break*)

enough money to keep me ·
in coffee and newspapers
and the occasional night out.
I know I'm poor but I can't get poverty right.
And she hugs me.
And there's beer in the refrigerator.
And, with three poems written in the past week,
I'm happy to be in my Hart Crane skin.
In a world of price tags,
I'm surprised at what I can afford.
The best things in life still aren't free
but most will take a deposit.

FIONA GRIMSHAW

James

Your death, my life.

I do not know you
James my brother.
Scarce two months old
You sleep your life away.
We almost meet
At grandmother's funeral;
They pull the earth away
And I can see you reach
To help her down.
Mother reminds me
Because you died, I live:
I am an intruder.
A strange love bonds us—
When I laugh
I laugh for two
And thank you for life
But when I weep
I weep for two
And wish that you had lived.

PIOTR GWIAZDA

Eternity, Etc.

*It was one of those metaphysical dirty words which no decent-minded man
would dream of pronouncing even to himself, much less in public. "Eternity,
my brethren." he said aloud. "Eternity, blah blah."*
--Aldous Huxley, *Island*

It took me all summer to read through *A Brief History of Time*
or rather it took me so long to understand it
and still certain details elude me: strong and weak forces,

the event horizon, black holes, dark matter, antimatter,
red giants, white dwarfs, wormholes—in short
the whole damn fairy tale… Oh yes, and the whole concept

of fourth dimension and time-space continuum:
I wonder, for example, if I read Proust in a space station
would I finish faster than reading him in my bed?

If I were a time traveler, could I visit Byzantium
as well as China? How to tell a black hole from just any hole?
And where does eternity fit (which scientists call *infinity*)?

If I believe in the Big Bang, do I also believe in the First Cause?
And that story about parallel worlds…what again
was my question? Well, these are all big questions—

something to think about when lifting weights at the gym
or making dinner for two on a weekend afternoon
(dinners, it occurs to me, taste best when they are made for two).

Take the "universe"—a unique, or not, accident in space
which then became time or vice versa.
We've counted fourteen billion years from the Big Xero

(I'd meant to say "Zero," but my pinky slipped on the keyboard
suggesting another idea: what if prehistory
is a malfunctioning copy machine; a budge, a hum, then light,

then everything goes berserk: globes, germs, genera spurt out--
one thing leads to another: light becomes air, air becomes water,
water becomes earth with dust on it, dust becomes man,

then man designs woman for his sick profit and pleasure--
but that's a different story. My point is (I'm
improvising) what if the script of human life is full of typos,

missteps, mishaps, false starts, false alarms,
wrong turns, dead ends, distractions, digressions--
in short, a palimpsest; at times it looks as if a monkey's typed it,

at times like a Shakespeare sonnet. Hence life is easy to chat
    about,
but difficult to explain. Hence luck, chance, coincidence
and all that blessed nonsense—Fate, Will, Eternity, etc...

So, when we look at the stars, at what they used to be
and presumably still are, this is not what we are likely to find:
all pieces fallen into place after the primal blow-up,

stars and planets with little flags fastened to them,
locations named, boundaries drawn, the whole universe mapped
    out
(maps, it occurs to me, are mirrors of clockwork consciousness).

No—it's still an undecided game: a throw of the dice,
which then breaks into billions of pieces, a tennis match
played with no ball, as at the close of *Blow Up*;

a scoreless game, a scoreless song; just deepening uncertainty
and silence, while the sleeping twins, space – time,
and their infant child God, shh...are having a dream about us.

JOHN HAINES

America

I keep trying to read
this book entitled *America.*

The author died five centuries ago,
a muddled dreamer
plotting the absurdities
of a hero who never reaches
the Western shore.

It is a story of blood
and dispossession,
of disenchantment because
one horizon never flowered
like the memory of another;
of waterholes watched
by laughing skulls,
prairies seeded with bones,
and clouds that refuse
to acknowledge the evening.

Perhaps it is not a book at all,
and I hold in my hands
a bundle of riddled pulp
saved from a shipwreck.

But it is the only book I have,
and I go on trying to read it;
at times exhausted, half-convinced
that neither the author,
the country or the hero,
ever existed.

--1964

JAMES HAUG

Scratch

Scratch is money, a form of bread.
Scratch is zero. A place to start from. To start
from scratch with scratch is easier
than to start from scratch without it.
Scratch is to scotch, end prematurely, as most
ends do. It's tough to scratch a project
that's amounted a serious pile of scratch.
No one wants to scratch that scratch.
Scratch is nothing, a form of dust. An end
and a beginning. A loan. Free publicity.
Scratch is what you must do if you don't
have scratch. Scratch out a living. A living
scratched is something else. A scribe can be
said to scratch. A line is scratched
about petals in Petaluma, but it's chicken
scratch. Scratch is to search, as when
a chicken scratches for feed. To scratch
around may turn up scratch, or bring
you vast amounts of scratch, or chicken feed,
which is very little scratch. A horse dropped
from the race is a scratch, and racing dailies
are scratch sheets. A scratch is a pocketed
cue-ball. In golf: no handicap. Spur of the moment,
a scratch band plays a honky-tonk
behind chicken-wire and, with luck, emerges
without a scratch. Beware: such scratch
efforts are seldom up to scratch. If
a scratcher says it's up to scratch, miles
above scratch, careful, it's empty flattery;
he'll want his back scratched in return.
A scratcher was a forger a hundred years ago.

(no stanza break)

125

He may have flopped in a scratch house.
A scratch hit is a fluke, lucky you, nearly
out at first, but safe. Scratch a surface
then find you've only scratched the surface.
A line is scratched, and you step over.

JAMES HAUG

Ghost 66

A mare's tail brushes over Indiana.
On Sunday, go-karts fly around
the figure-eight. Plywood Arc de Triomphe
and a cyclone fence. Powerlines make
a margin at the bottom of the sky—a staff,
Little Birds, and you are the notes
when the wind comes, and it does.
If we could only harness such power,
dreams the cook at Steak 'n' Shake.
It could happen. He saw tray girls,
and there were tray girls, roller skates
on the lone prairie, and lunch came sailing
over fresh macadam with a smile.
It's no mirage, stranger, this dirt is
a town. Gaze out the picture window,
picture where you're headed: the horizon,
then more horizon, swallowed by dusk.
Then more horizon.

CAROLINE HEMPHILL

Dear/ darling/

how surprised I was/to come home/to your note/
a chalk outline/on the living/room floor/the dishes
still in the sink/Capone/carried/a pistol/in his golf bag/
shot/himself/in/the/foot/a good caddie/makes all/
the difference/Lancelot/rode two horses/to death/
trying/to get to Guinevere/in a blizzard/follow/
the brake lights/of strangers/the theme/of the novel/is
people are wretched/to each/other/to make a proper pie
crust/ice the butter/cut into flour/a knife/in each/hand/
roll it out/not too thin/or you/ll have holes/in the dough/
what you fill it with/says a/lot/about whether you/d/be
the sort of chap/one/d/want in a foxhole/or/whether
you/d/piss/your/self/to make an explosive device/pour
in/blasting powder/insert/a fuse/the novel/considers/
the point of view of/the four/and twenty/black/birds/
imprisoned/in the pie/leopards go for/the jugular/
baboons/flip their prey/on their backs/rip the guts out/
we could have been/a sonnet/we could/have been/
a revolution/

WILLIAM HEYEN

Affliction

On August 17, 1940, Adam
Czerniakow, Chairman
of Warsaw's *Judenrat*,
visited the sanatorium
at Otwock.
He tells us in his diary
of being accosted
by a fellow Jew who
believed himself afflicted
with black candles
inside his body.

We see these, now,
from this far,
their flames
gusting inside him
black as the light
behind the killers' eyes.
How numerous these candles!
But they cannot,
no matter
how long they burn,
burn their way to surface

for Czerniakow the suicide
even after death.
The stricken ones—these eyes,
these candles that see
into us as though we were
instinct with them,
as though we could have helped

(no stanza break)

129

the candled ones,
&, the next time,
which will surely come,
will.

WILLIAM HEYEN

Candy

All we could do was to remember it, to deal in our memories, to create out of them poems and stories, history and reminiscences. It was the only way through which that irrevocably destroyed past could survive. Vilna had once been a red giant star in the firmament and had once illuminated the Jewish universe. It had now been extinguished. It had become a white dwarf star, emitting a feeble light visible only to those who knew of its existence.

Lucy S. Dawidowicz

I dreamed I worked in a shop in old Vilna,
there again this dim morning for the thousandth time.
First the boiling of sugar & milk in a large cauldron
over an open fire, then the stirring in of fruit syrups
with a wooden paddle. Was it you who helped me
carry the cauldron to a trough, & pour?

We kneaded the smoky mixture with our smoking hands,
then pushed it into a metal roller. Then the cutter.
That's all I remember, except for a huge map hanging
in the heavens, festooned with hundreds of tiny bulbs
where Jews had lived for centuries. The bulbs blinked
on & off for a while, then one by one blinked off....

We taste them we taste them again, we taste them
we taste them again, we cannot not taste them but
for how long O we are among the last we
taste them we cannot not taste them their
living sweetness in this air with our tongues we
taste them in this dreamed dim light of old Vilna....

You had left me. Where were you? Were you there?

(*no stanza break*)

131

I woke with the taste of red & green candies
in my mind, & in my chest a loss of light
sweet beyond redeeming—all that was left, for now,
of that city, until our next passage over cobblestones
through the feeble starlight of old Vilna.

WILLIAM HEYEN

Almond

Herr Professor Doktor Heyen,
meine Name ist Maria Mandel,
SS, Auschwitz. I place myself here
in your imaginings by free will
to speak something from where
I have pulsed and circled in starlight
for what seems a thousand years,
or no time at all. *Mandel,*
yes, I'm almond—and as a child
I loved *Kuchen* with honeyed
slices of almond, as though, yes,
my surname were prophecy and fate.
Yes, I led children to the gas,
sometimes caressed the cutest
to calm them, but prodded
the frightened ones to speed them
to their Jewish state, their god
in the clouds, their palestine.
Did I lose sleep? For these
not worth whatever cost
the Reich incurred in bluish pellets
or injections of cyanide,
that bitter almond?
Herr Doktor, with your education,
surely I'm within your understanding:
the children would have grown
into more than harmless vermin.
We unsung heroines ask to be forgiven
only our incompletions...until we return
like almond trees in spring,
so beautiful and thirsty
to resume our destiny again.

WILLIAM HEYEN

Kindred Spirits

In that Wagnerian opera of the Fuhrer's mind—
we hide in timewells as forces transpire—
mobs sing in chorus, soldiers march by torchlight,
Nordic heroes move the audience to tears.
We cower & pray, but it's no use, he finds us out,

we who are not blond as dogs
who tear at our smothered in their synagogues
for the fat that runs in channels cut in dirt
out from under corpsewood pyres
composed with such love for mankind & for nature.

JANE HIRSHFIELD

The Opening

Every meeting is fateful.

A bot fly lays her yellow eggs on the leg of a horse.

A door latch slips into place
and the story once told behind it is over:

A sentence turns in mid-stride and
becomes a question.

No one knows why.

But mostly we keep on asking.
A sound like many small birds in a tree.
A sound like rain.

Once, in the long midsummer drought
of coastal California, I heard a sound that puzzled.
I went outside to stars,
my outstretched hand unwetted.

But from every tree around me, water came hard,
the downpour still at full in its falling.

The gutters made the sound they throat while working.
My hand was dry.

I stood inside the mystery,
no question in my heart's fast beating.

JOHN HODGEN

Coast to Coast

Art Bell takes another call.
A woman with a voice like rain beginning its lonely song
says she sees people standing at the far edges of her eyes,
just outside her peripheral vision, never there when she looks,
but always at the sides. Shadow people, she calls them,
like angels or aliens walking among us.
I think of Tom Joad walking home from prison,
standing at the edge of his Dust Bowl farm
before going inside to his mother,
who sees him out of the corner of her eye
like a shadow she always knew would be there.
I think of the squadron of pilots lost in the Bermuda Triangle
coming home to their families, like ghosts at the edge
of the lawn, extra uncles at the family reunion,
someone standing in a photograph who shouldn't be there,
the thirteenth disciple, the fourth musketeer.

When the woman is finished the phone lines light up,
an army of callers who say the same thing,
that they see these people, standing like saints,
like the Sergeant Pepper cover,
like deer at the edge of a clearing.

I see them too.
My neighbor to the left of me, walking in her yard
like Emily Dickinson alone in the world,
or Venus de Milo missing her arms.

My neighbor to the right,
the old woman gone deaf since her husband has died,
her TV so loud all the neighbors can hear,
the laugh track lifting up in the night like a chorus for us all.

If the scientists are right,
our images rise into space that way, endlessly,
like shadows standing at the edge of God's eyes.
If we could outdistance light, get out ahead of it somehow,
we could look down and see ourselves, our pasts,
our second grade class, the little haloes on our heads,
or lonely Abe Lincoln tugging at his beard,
John Wilkes Booth coming up out of the corner of his eye.
We could see our own shadow people standing beside us,
Methuselah, Dante, Mr. Bojangles,
and Garbo and Mozart and Hedy Lamarr,
and Harpo and Jesus, Art Bell and his callers,
and someone stepping forward from the chorus on the shore,
your mother perhaps, beginning to speak,
her voice like the first drops of rain.

JOHN HODGEN

For the Young Man Who Would Not Let Me in to Visit Keat's Grave with Ten Minutes Left Until Closing Time at the Cimitero Accatolica, Rome, December 1ˢᵗ, 2002

He knew what he knew. Not stubborn exactly, not sullen, nor stupid,
just a boy turning slowly into a man, as if a key were turning softly
   inside a lock,
as if today he had stepped forward forever into the way he will be in this
   world.
This day he was simply pledging allegiance to the closing of the gate,
yet he knew a little already about the way things work in this place,
the way at three o'clock in the afternoon, even earlier sometimes,
the light begins to lose its hope, descend its cross,
the way the day gives up the ghost, drifts freely out to sea.

And he was gainfully employed, a digger of graves, as I was even before
   his age,
and he knew even then that it was better somehow when the others
   were gone.
And he wouldn't take money, wouldn't see in my hand or eyes
any reason for giving away the hard-won currency of his own free time,
so late in my life, so late in his day.

Today I am convinced he had a lover waiting, a girl, moody and
   forward,
his own Fanny Brawne, and he ached for her, truly, made in her his own
   grave.
And he weighed every moment it would take him to reach her,
past the rusty pyramid of Caius Cestius, past Monte Testaccio,
past the neighboring cemetery of the English war dead,
past the seedy nightclubs Latina and Radio London, sleepy now

in the afternoon light, where punkers will gather to rave until morning,
ignorant and beautiful, while he and his girlfriend lie sleeping together,
breathing their silence, freely, effortlessly,
like wind in the graveyard, words on the sea,
the two of them drifting through the gates of the other.

JOHN HODGEN

Word Search

My mother, before her stroke, took up doing puzzles that came each
    month
like quiet guests she would greet with a smile, simple word games
    mostly,
fill-in-the-blanks, that offered prize money if you made the final round.

Only there never was a final round. There were quarter-finals, semi-
    finals,
winners' circles, trophy rounds, various and sundry tournaments of
    champions,
each with more games, each costing more money, each easily
    recognizable,
perhaps even to her, as scams, as pathetic, egregious, niggling schemes.

But she never let on, kept sending for more, along with the money
she sent televangelists, lost animal shelters, Readers' Digest book clubs,
black starving children sitting next to a bowl, their dark eyes sunk
like lost pennies into their heads, their tiny hands at the sides of their
    faces,
as if they were solving the world's hardest puzzle.

And she was good at them, though they seemed easy to me, hard only
    to imagine
how someone could miss them, a stripper turned waitress outside Reno
    perhaps,
thinking NOME for a four-letter city in Alaska, while her husband,
    emphysemic,
at the end of the trailer yelled JUNO, Goddamnit, JUNO, the woman
    with her hand
at the side of her face, caught for a moment, like a lost animal,
between a word she once knew, and the place she was in.

And maybe my mother was good at them because of her husbands, two
    puzzles
themselves, my father who died without any insurance, her losing the
    house,
marrying again, a man, emphysemic, who looked like Shemp Howard,

who smoked in his chair by his oxygen tank, and argued with Alex
   Trebek.

After her stroke my brother and I wrote DECEASED on her junk mail,
   sending it back,
knowing with each word we were killing her again, though she lay still
   alive, mostly,
she and her stunted arm, in a nursing home in Manchester, New
   Hampshire,
cold as Alaska, her books stacked up, her cross in her hand, her eyes
   sunken pennies,
looking lost, slightly puzzled, her life having turned into a word she did
   not know.

CYNTHIA MARIE HOFFMAN

The Athletic Heartbeat
for David

> All real living is meeting.
> --Martin Buber, *I and Thou*

Ladies and gentlemen, you are assembled here tonight
to recoup a common squandry. Quietly

please, without calling attention to yourselves,
turn your heads to the left, and find the man

slim as a straw with the long hair slung on his back
like a rug drying out in the sun. You can't miss him.

His hands are in his lap—we have come at a good time—
and the left one, palm up, may look the hand of a beggar,

but it is the hand of an athlete. We will be the only ones
who notice him measuring his pulse like this, at midnight,

in a crowded room. Look now, he takes a refill on his drink,
the universal drink of bears and crows: melted snow.

This man may not look familiar, but you have all
met him. For example, the older man in the back

with the parrot-blue bow tie, you have yelled
obscenities at him on the street. And you, the lady

in the mini-skirt up front, you shouldered him so hard
on your way to the ladies' room in a bar like this one

that long after you'd snapped the lipstick cap on
like a disjointed finger back into its place

and carefully pressed your mouth on a paper towel
in front of the dimly lit mirror, the rush of heat

was still spreading outward through the long palm leaf of his
    triceps.
This was only a couple weeks ago. But it's likely you don't
    remember.

It's likely none of you remember.
Those of you who shook his hand don't remember

whether it was wide or calloused. Those of you who didn't
shake his hand don't remember why. Who among you

can name the scar in his eyebrow, shaped like
a "V," a stealth bomber, open scissor blades, migrating

geese, the way we spread our fingers apart
meaning *peace*? Who knows that at eleven, still a boy,

he lay in his bed with his eyes open, and the gray-white walls
    around him
were the gray-white stem of the mushroom cloud

that would at any moment indisputably end the Cold War?
But don't misunderstand. The true misfortune

is not that you have all been speeding through your lives,
not that you haven't invited him out for burgers or flapjacks,

interviewed him for his personal history or studied the deep-set
    crease in his cheeks.
The true misfortune, ladies and gentlemen,

is not that you haven't felt your own hand in his,
but that you haven't felt him feeling your hand.

That you do not daily remind yourselves
that the bomb never went off, not for real. Not in that boy's
    room

or in your own. That at midnight in a crowded room
you are not also taking your own pulse.

I will be your tour guide. In a minute we will approach the bar
in a single file line, and every one of you will pass this man again.

Only this time, I ask as you move behind him,
press your forehead to the cool drape of his hair and breathe
    deeply

the coconut and papaya. He will feel you breathing, note
the sensation of molecules laden with scent leaving him. I ask
    that you feel him

feeling the pull of your lungs. Ladies and gentlemen,
slowly now. The athletic heart beats only forty-four times a
    minute.

And for those of you still guessing, that scar in his eyebrow
is the deeply forked tail of the barn swallow.

She darts from rafter to rafter like an atom
through the space that is the only difference between us.

HILARY HOLLIDAY

The Horsemen

> My heart skipped within me thinking they had been Englishmen,
> … but when they came near, there was a vast difference
> between the lovely faces of Christians, and the foul looks of
> those heathens.
>> --*The Narrative of the Captivity and Restoration of Mrs. Mary
>> Rowlandson* (1682)

They had finally crossed the Baquag,
thirty or so Englishmen in fine attire,
hats bobbing in sunlight, sashes flying,
radiant horses triumphing over the open field.
I clapped my hands, cried out praise to God.
Hope filled the space where hunger was;
if they were coming, then surely I was going
home.

Imagine, if you will, the rainy darkness,
the chill wind in my heart, when I saw them
for what they were, a company of Indians
dressed in English clothes. It was then
I looked down at my raw hands, my ragged sleeves,
and saw them in *me*: fellow imposter
tricked out like their starving
kin.

Some watery firmament caused us
to materialize in each other's eyes,
mirrored emissaries of God's encrypted plan.
It would take a captive more brilliant than I
to break the divine code of those noisome days;
to determine in a moment's glad, thundering arrival
which foul look to snub, which lovely face to
recognize.

HILARY HOLLIDAY

There Lie Their Clothes

> ...as I was eating[,] another Indian said to me: He seems to be
> your good friend, but he killed two Englishmen at Sudbury and
> there lie their clothes behind you. I looked behind me and there
> I saw bloody clothes with bullet holes in them.
> > --*The Narrative of the Captivity and Restoration of Mrs. Mary*
> > *Rowlandson* (1682)

I saw blood on a white shirt, yes,
    but also sweat from a stranger's strivings:

chopping and stacking, then hurrying
    to the fire-flashed window to shoot against the light.

And I saw reddened trousers full of holes but
    otherwise neat and well-pressed, thanks to a wife's good
care;

a scarf and gloves much nicer than my husband's;
    and beside all that,

a top coat with shiny buttons, burr-covered stockings,
    a ticking heirloom on a tangled chain.

Had the owners of these clothes tipped hats, touched hands,
    walked shadow upon shadow down the streets of Sudbury?

Was there faith between them?
    Could they be brothers?

No matter, now.
    In the wigwam, I watched their clothes grow easy,

slouching and dozing in the tobacco-filled air.
It made no difference where

they hung or fell, now that they had begun the long
anticipated journey

back to fiber and ore, mud and stem.

HILARY HOLLIDAY

Dining with Weetamoo

A severe and proud dame she was; bestowing every day, in
dressing herself neat, as much time as any of the gentry of the
land, powdering her hair and painting her face, going with
necklaces, with jewels in her ears, and bracelets upon her hands.
   --*The Narrative of the Captivity and Restoration of Mrs. Mary
   Rowlandson* (1682)

Strange sister, dark twin, my first and only mistress,
we have walked side by side all day,
and I have seen you lift your skirts
to navigate rocks and briars;
I have felt your sheet of shiny hair
snap against my face.
Now you are eating boiled squirrel,
not sharing, making me watch.
Blood drips down your chin
onto the blouse I sewed for you
without your asking me to.
You have never liked my gifts,
not since Philip offered me his hand
when we crossed the Baquag
and left you to wade through
the iced current on your own.
Now both he and your husband
are gone, and you have no idea
when, or with whom, they will return.

Where does your mind take you, sitting there,
clutching a dead squirrel's gray plume?
Do you imagine yourself English,
wearing lace instead of deerskin,

(no stanza break)

148

attending a ball?
Would you like to take my life and try it on?
I remember, you know, the day the warriors
came back from Northampton,
discouraged, not bearing much,
and you snatched away their bundles,
sorted through them till you found a dress like mine.
Your cheeks glowed when you emerged from the wigwam,
a haughty dame in crisp, clean layers.
I turned and laughed behind my hand:
You had it buttoned wrong.

Or maybe there is more to you
and your mind has settled on your dead child,
the heart stab we share but never speak of.
The night he died, I stayed with other Indians
who gave me a skin to rest on.
I could hear your wails curling
around the tiny leaves of spring,
entering the smoky space
where the smell of venison
made my companions smile.
The next morning, your friends came
to howl your baby into whatever mist
you imagine as your Heaven.
Their cries filled the blue, pure air;
I stood apart and stared at a blur
of tiny flowers on the softened ground,
the shadow of a robin.
The sun warmed all our heads,
and in the secret world behind my eyes,
my own lost child came to me, laughing,
running across the yard in Lancaster,
her hands full of daffodils.

That evening, believing your pain
no more or less than mine,
I brought you peas, a cup of broth,

(no stanza break)

and yes, it hurt my feelings when
you ignored my gift and walked outside.
But I ate the peas, swallowed down the drink,
slept well and long, cheek pressed
to my Bible, legs stretched out at last.
In the morning, when you came back,
looked pointedly at the empty dish and cup,
your lips a tight, hard line,
I did not say *I'm sorry.*

Now it is weeks later, and we are in Nichewaug,
under a pale-green maple tree,
and you have finally given me a morsel of squirrel.
I am smiling, saying *thank you,*
as if we were ladies conversing over tea
and this were delectable, and the truth is, it is.
In just a few hours,
we will resume our travels;
we will again walk side by side,
my strange sister, my dark twin,
you with your burdens and I with mine.

KARLA M. HUSTON

Burying the Red Shoes: Conversations with Four Poets

Last summer, I found myself sitting before the computer, the only one at Ragdale with Internet access. Ragdale is an artist and writers' retreat in Lake Forest, Illinois, and I'd received a month-long residency, ostensibly to write the introductory chapters for my Master of Arts thesis. My subject: the nature of risk-taking and women's writing.

I sent an email note to Denise Duhamel, who had become a friend after a workshop I attended at the Iowa Summer Writing Festival a couple of summers before. "Will you talk to me about women's writing and risk?" I asked. She readily agreed. So I sent twelve questions (formed early in my writing process) dealing with what I thought to be the nature of risk in writing: how to say the unsayable "Saying the unsayable" was a mantra repeated by every writing teacher with whom I'd ever studied. What did it mean exactly? I wanted clarification. And I thought perhaps women writers took different kinds of risks.

Duhamel generously answered my questions. So did Naomi Shihab Nye, a friend of a friend and a woman whose writing I often used in the creative writing classes I teach. A few weeks after speaking online with Nye, I made an email request to Shara McCallum, a poet who'd done a short writer-in-residence at the University of Wisconsin Oshkosh the year before. I thought, with her Afro-Jamaican, Venezuelan background, she might have something different to add. Finally, I remembered Stellasue Lee, the poetry editor of *RATTLE*, had once told me fewer women writers submitted poems to the journal. I wondered if that were still true and if she would be willing to answer some questions about risk taking. She graciously agreed.

Now I had twelve questions and a series of responses from four women writers whose work I admired and respected. When I formatted each poet's answers, the disparate email interviews became one. The finished product read like these women had been sitting at my kitchen table and talking to me about writing while I poured coffee and passed the cream and sugar.

Huston: What are some of the greatest risks faced by writers writing today?

Nye: You know, I can't really speak for other writers. But I guess writers have always shared a risk of not being understood, of being misunderstood, of having words taken out of context or exploited for someone else's purposes. But these are risks worth taking. I think the risk of not speaking, of living in a box of containment, would feel much greater.

Duhamel: I think the confessional poets risk "confessing" too much. By that, I don't mean REVEALING too much but rather revealing without using interesting language, sophistication in tone or form or irony. Shock for shock value can be as boring as an uneventful poem.

McCallum: Probably being more focused on their career than on their writing. I don't know that this hasn't always been a source of distraction for writers, but I think the tendency of writers (especially poets) to be centralized in academia increases the "careerist" impulses. At least I've been ‚witnessing this a lot with fellow writers and even my students, whose first thoughts are too often about where they'll publish and what prizes they'll win rather than if the work is any good. I think it's easy to succumb to the pressures to publish and to get caught up in believing the hype around the "famous" poet, but in the end that can't be what matters most. I try very hard to remind myself of what really counts -- which for me is to write as well as I can -- and to surround myself with like-minded individuals.

Lee: Saying the unsayable. And, once said, isn't there something that has to be done?

Huston: Are the risks greater for women writers?

Nye: I don't think so. Never did. Others might think so.

Duhamel: For women writers, these risks are exponential. We're used to read[ing] war stories about heroic men, but think of the backlash of women who choose to write about incest, infidelity, and so on. They are usually met with literary scorn since people in general and men specifically feel so uncomfortable around those topics. [It's the] same with

152

people of color. In *Ploughshares*, [Cornelius Eady] writes in his introduction how often black poets are asked *not* to write "political" poems in traditional workshops--well, their very lives are political.

McCallum: Well, not the risks that I've just outlined above [focus on career, pressure to publish]. There may be other risks that women face more often. If I had to say which ones seem specific to women, it would come down to the choice of subject matter. Even while things have changed, there's still a tendency to privilege a male position and male experience as "universal." I think the same is true with minority versus majority subjects or points of view.

Lee: Yes, because of the roles of women, which with all the changes, still haven't changed that much. When given a vote, men vote with their feet—women, as a rule, are left with what the men walk away from. Also, in a recent issue of *RATTLE*, when asked by Alan Fox, my publisher: Do you think there's any essential difference between male poets and female poets? Lucille Clifton says:

> Male poets have wives. That's significant, because they have somebody who will watch the kids, who do the work, the grunt work, who will give them time, allow them time. I've had males get mad at me about that but the fact is, generally, I have seen female poets do it all and then still write poems. There was an old Peanuts cartoon once where Lucy was talking to Snoopy about this. I think he said, "What do wives do?" She told him, and he said, "I gotta get me one of those." Other than that, subject matter, but superficial things. But I think they tend to have time.

Huston: Is risk-taking always telling secrets?

Nye: Not at all. Risk-taking means extending beyond the self in some way, making oneself available or visible or accessible to others -- then living with the consequences. Which are usually good, by the way!

Duhamel: Risk-taking is much more than telling secrets. It's having an opinion, a stand on an issue, especially an unpopular stand.

McCallum: No. Taking a risk in a poem requires you to be vulnerable and have something at stake. I think this is what makes all writing -- not just poems -- any good: that is, I think we are most invested in a piece when we believe the writer is also invested and has something at stake personally in the piece. This is not synonymous with confession of deep, dark secrets, however. In fact, I think there are many writers who reveal secrets in ways that feel anything but personally risky, in ways that seem calculated and exploitative of the event. To the contrary, there are writers like Adrienne Rich who try to write about events outside of their own lives in ways that feel very risky to me. I don't think Rich is always successful, but I admire the risks she takes very much. I don't mean to imply that telling a personal secret might not be a risk-taking gesture, just that I don't believe it always is.

Lee: No, it's saying it like it is, and "like it really is" is one big fat secret.

Huston: Is risk-taking always sexual?

Nye: Not at all! I was personally never very interested in writing about anything sexual, but I didn't mind reading about that subject at all if others wrote about it! Who knows, I may start tomorrow!"

Duhamel: No--I think risk-taking can have to do with the political and the social. In Cornelius Eady's book *Brutal Imagination*, he writes from the point of view of the man Susan Smith said kidnapped and drowned her kids. Of course, that man DOESN'T exist and that makes the poems that much more brilliant. Ai also writes in the voice of Jeffrey Dahmer and so on.

McCallum: No. It can be a risk to say something sexual, but again I don't think it's always the case that saying something sexual is risky, and I especially don't think that the only way to take a risk is to write about sexuality.

Lee: Heavens no.

Huston: What other kinds of risks might women writers take?

Nye: Being controlled by others seems like a much greater risk to

154

me. Not speaking up would be a devastating risk. Of shrinkage.

Duhamel: Women risk being judged by the subject matter of their poetry rather than its artistry.

McCallum: I think writing itself is a risk when done as if you are sitting on the edge of your seat. If you say something that you are unsure about, that's when you take risks.

Lee: To study craft, what a concept, right? Yes, not just to take a pretty pen and some quality paper, but to study, read, think, take apart, put it together again.

Note: Lee told me that as poetry editor of RATTLE, she would publish more women writers, but fewer women writers submitted. When I asked Lee recently if this were still true, she said that the overwhelming number of submissions to Rattle came from male writers. When I asked her why, she said:

Women think poetry is supposed to be hearts and flowers. They don't seem to read as much; they just like to write, and we have been the peace makers for so long that hearts and flowers seem to be the most accessible part of ourselves. I was the keynote speaker and ran a workshop for Perie Longo [poetry therapist and marriage, family and child therapist] in Santa Barbara this summer. I took participants through an exercise that resulted in a twenty-minute writing period to see what they came up with. It was not a random exercise, but I told them exactly what to do to get started. Out of about thirty in the class of which most were women, some fifteen have not submitted their work [to *RATTLE*], even though I have called them personally; Perie has called them personally, TWICE. I was at a workshop a couple of Sundays ago for the National Association of Healing Poetry, and one of the women from Perie's workshop was there, and I asked why she hadn't submitted. She told me she didn't think her work was good enough--that SHE was just "fooling around" with her writing. I'm afraid I lost it. I told her that she had no right to pass judgment on her work; she wasn't the editor, I WAS!

Note: When I asked Lee what she meant by women writing "hearts and flowers," she replied:

155

I mean not writing the truth, but rather soft-soaping it, taking the cutting edge out of it. I knew an Episcopal priest who gave this sermon over and over again: "It's wrong to commit adultery, but sometimes we find ourselves in difficult situations." In other words, it's wrong, but then maybe it's OK. This is called a double message. It can't be one way and another as well. There are a lot of grays in the world. Why isn't the work of women as powerful as that of men? Men seem to have far different values about what is their black and white.

Huston: *Are you aware when you take a risk with subject, structure, and language—as in "I'll probably get into trouble for saying this"?*

Nye: No. You feel as if you're having more fun than usual.

Duhamel: No, unfortunately not. Well, maybe fortunately not. I never censor myself until the poem's done, and I see what I have.

McCallum: Sometimes. Right now I'm working on a poem sequence that has to do with political events in Jamaica during the 1970s. This is a subject that will, in some ways, question the complicity of the US government (via the CIA), the Jamaican government (via the two political parties who were in power during that decade), and even the Jamaican people in a series of violent and inhumane events. I don't know that I'll "get into trouble" in any real fashion (most poets aren't prosecuted for their beliefs other than by other poets who may write nasty reviews; I'm thinking of the response to Carolyn Forché's work here; and I can live with that kind of "trouble"). But the subject feels risky to me in a more deeply personal way. I don't know if I can get it right precisely because it was so complicated a situation, and it's a time period about which there are conflicting reports -- and I was only a child while it was all going on. Most people would also rather forget these events than address them, it seems to me. So, I'm aware that there's risk here of people not understanding why I would stir up the past, but I believe in this project and ultimately am choosing not to let the potential for censure stop me.

Lee: No, I made up my mind years and years ago about this. I wrote about my husband and after, when he said to me why not flowers and trees, I said to him, "And, you are always free to change my experience!" I tell my students all the time, ALL THE TIME, to write it like it is. I mean, what are the chances that one's mother or one's father or one's husband will ever see what we've written if it is published -- unless our ego says, "Oh, lookie here, see, I'm published." We need approval so much we can't say the unsayable because then, then, then, where would we get the approval we need from? And, nobody, NOBODY has given us the permission to say the unsayable.

Huston: *Who are or have been your risk-taking role models?*

Nye: So many poets! Most poets! Henry David Thoreau, Jack Kerouac, Joni Mitchell, Tom Waits.

Duhamel: Sharon Olds, Ai, Kathleen Spivak.

McCallum: Adrienne Rich, Louise Glück, Eavan Boland, Lucille Clifton.

Lee: One thing I learned putting on the *RATTLE* reading series with the likes of C.K. Williams, Charles Simic, Stephen Dobyns, Sharon Olds, Lucille Clifton, Gerald Stern, on and on with the names already and every one of them just wanted to know if they were OK. Did they do a good job and did the audience like them? We are all looking for approval.

Huston: *What women writers are taking great risks today?*

Nye: All of them.

Duhamel: I think many women writers are taking risks -- some with books, some whose work I come across in magazines. I just read an amazing first book by Betsy Brown called *A Year of Morphines: Poems,* about losing her mother and sister to breast cancer and her father to pancreatic cancer. I mean, I can imagine a publisher saying who wants to read THAT? Well, I did. And others too -- it won the National Poetry Series and was published by LSU. It has dazzling, confrontational, raging, subject matter AND the poems are artful and amazing.

McCallum: Same as above.

Lee: We all are, some of us, better than others.

Huston: In an online interview Sharon Olds is credited as being "fearless ... a writer who sees heroism in the everyday." Yet she has been criticized for being too "out there." What do you think?

Nye: I don't know what too "out there" means.

Duhamel: I think people who criticize Sharon Olds are more often than not freaked out by her subject matter but don't say so. Instead the reviews talk about a sloppy line break here and an imperfect title there. I'm not saying that everyone need like Sharon Olds' work, but I hardly ever read a smart review against it.

McCallum: I'm often surprised by the hoopla surrounding Olds since it doesn't seem to me that her poems are "out there" or that risky even in a contemporary context. Given the harsh and often vitriolic response by many in the poetry--particularly male--establishment to her work, though I think she must be hitting a nerve. Poetry in particular still seems controlled by rather conservative notions when it comes to what is "acceptable" subject matter for a poet. (i.e., you can write about trees but not vaginas; or if you want to write about the latter, you can only do it only indirectly and preferably only if you are male).

Lee: I loved meeting Sharon Olds. My God, to think that anyone would criticize any of us ... who has the right to make those kinds of judgments? Certainly not me.

Huston: How do you contend with poems about family members or people who might be close to you?

Nye: Good question. I don't always show them the poems. I don't always publish them. But I write them.

Duhamel: I don't show them my poems! Honestly. And they don't want to see them. We have a don't-ask-don't-tell kind of policy in my family. I've shown my parents my work in the past, and they were so freaked out/hurt/angry that we just called a truce. I saw Erica Jong on a television interview with her daughter (who is now also a novelist) and the daughter said she was creeped out by her mother's imagination (the sex stuff) and Erica was always very hurt by that. But now that her daughter is writing, Erica is also freaked out to read her daughter's stuff. So maybe there is this taboo in place -- we don't really want to enter the heads of our parents or children in that way. I wish it were different in my family, but they don't read Sharon Olds or Ai or any other contemporary poets either -- so it's hard for them to put me in context. And why should they have to? I don't write to communicate with my family.

McCallum: I don't worry about this as much with poetry as I do with the nonfiction I write. For one thing, even while my poems are partly autobiography (sometimes even totally so), I don't see them as mimetic with my life and experience. Also, poems are far more slippery in terms of meaning, so it's easier for people (especially those who the poem may be based on) to read themselves in a way that they find satisfactory. My mother's response to my first book -- if this gives you any indication -- was of how "nice" it was and hers was the response I most feared. Even if I've written a poem that indicts someone for something he or she has done -- as I do at times with the poems based on my relationship with my mother -- I'd hope in the end that the picture of the person I offer up is complex enough that I don't reduce him or her to a villain. Ultimately, the measures of a good poem – morally/ethically and aesthetically -- are not in opposition to me. If a poem succeeds, its main intent is not to injure or be at someone else's expense. As Annie Dillard says, and I fully agree, "Literature is an art, not a martial art."

Lee: I remember when I just started writing. There was a class reading at the literary center in Venice, California, and I read a poem that even I had not a clue what this poem was really about, the statement it made, and after, my then husband, came up to me and said, "What's wrong with you? Why can't you be like other women and write about flowers and trees?" I write it, publish it, and bury my need for approval in the garden along with my red shoes that I loved so much I couldn't stand to throw them away.

Huston: If you pull back as a writer and don't write about the things that disturb you or even bring you joy — for fear of hurting someone — isn't that really self-censorship? Is self-censoring sometimes necessary?

Nye: Yes. I think it's very necessary. But again, one need not publish everything one writes. "Self-censorship" sounds negative, but "being a filter" for what we choose to write and the ways we write it sounds more promising. We can all be filters for whatever we say or want to say and how we say it. But again, one need not publish everything one writes. It's necessary to write to discover what we do and don't want to write, and we grow more empowered to decide those things AS we write, not before.

Duhamel: No. I think you MUST write the poem. You really must. Whether you choose to publish it is another matter. I think it's perfectly fine to put certain poems in a drawer or file or safety deposit box.

McCallum: You can write anything you want, and I do. The question really becomes, should you censor yourself in what you publish. I think you should. It's a bit vain to think that everything you've written needs to see the light of day anyway. When it comes down to publishing a piece or not, then I ask myself what I would lose and gain by doing so? If it would really hurt someone I cared about, I haven't published it. To my mind, anyway, I have not done that.

Lee: It's worse than just self-censorship. It's chopping yourself off at the knees. Say there is a whole very long line of people out in the world to beat me up. I'm not going to push them all out of the way to get to the front of the line to beat myself up. It's time to get off that fence, ladies, time to say it like it is.

Huston: Are you ever afraid that you've crossed the line, gone too far?

Nye: Nope. I don't see a line.

Duhamel: No. I want to go further. Honestly, I really do.

McCallum: I think I just answered this above, but I'll say that the line I've established for myself is one I don't feel I've crossed. Everyone has a different "line," though. I can only give you my sense of it and hope that I'm not letting myself off the hook. I ask myself these kinds of questions a lot, which is maybe my only assurance that I'm trying to be not only a good writer but a good person.

160

Lee: I don't give it any thought whatsoever.

Final Note: Michelle Berth, one of my high school students, was so taken by Duhamel's poetry that I encouraged her to make contact and tell her so. She asked her: "Are you ever worried that any of your poems will 'cross the line' in subject matter, or is there no barrier whatsoever when you write?"

Duhamel: Yes, this is something that I think about a lot! There are only about three poems I've written so far that I just feel I cannot responsibly publish because they would hurt too many people. But for the most part, I try to get my work out there, as uncomfortable as it may be. I heard Sharon Olds speak once about taboo in writing. She said when you write a poem that you know will potentially harm someone and you put in your drawer, it's a little suicide. When you send it out into the world, it's a little murder. Neither one feels great, but that is the downside to being a writer.

HOLLY IGLESIAS

Sister,

I fear that we may lose him. He hangs by a thread, mumbling, fitful, refusing beef tea, porridge, not even a slice of bread.

They found him by the Egyptian Temple, a Jefferson Guard actually carried him into the parlor, oh such lovely gold braid across his chest, a rather tall fellow. Well. Yes, found him on the Pike, eating peanuts from a paper sack. In shirtsleeves, my God, no hat. I suspect he wanted a stroll; business has not been good. But he knows his nerves.

What will we tell mother? You know I have cared for him, kept my tongue as Rose blows off to her reform club, which is as sorry an excuse for a nice luncheon in your new hat as I've ever seen.

Nonetheless. Sister, our dear brother was too weak for the fair. It has taken its toll and who is accountable? A man who suffers from coffee heart has no place in a wild wamboozle of tambourines and googaws and swimming elephants and harem girls.

Finish with the beans and squash, dear, but come when you can, oh do come soon.

HOLLY IGLESIAS

Hygienics

A standing menace, surely, this fouled pond of humanity. Unmentionable, impolite as boils or venereal fever. You can see them—stacked by the coal chute, staring blankly, a basket of babies under a decrepit stair. Filthy sink, no privy, heaps of rubbish, bodies, rags, sewage leaking from the pipes. The whites of their eyes float in darkness.

A bath house is needed.

An incinerator would do a world of good.

HOLLY IGLESIAS

Flossie & TR

Arms akimbo, eyes smiling beneath a flirtatious hat, she
waits at Station 7. It is May. Her month: May for nosegays and
Mother Mary, for sun-warmed hair in a stylish roll resting on
the nape of her neck. For worrying rascal tendrils between her
fingers.

Jacket trim, skirts   ample, the cotton lawn of her waist
starched into submission. On her lap, *Sonnets from the
Portuguese*, a prop like her swan-head umbrella. She has only
time and a convent education of little use when the destination
is the Tyrolean beer garden and a beau with two left feet.

A carriage passes.

And in it she sees the glare of a monocle, that enormous mouth
of teeth. Trained upon her, a palpable gaze as he tips his hat in
her direction, the color rising in her face, spite banging in her
breast as she refuses him a smile.

HOLLY IGLESIAS

Too Long at the Fair

I am the medicine, the cure worse than pain. Here. Let me feed
you as I scold, feed you Igorots and Negritos on a spoon, tiny
peoples who trip over our tongue, amusing us no end with
stammers and clicks, the brown brown diet of root and dog, less
refined than our pink spun sugar and veal chops. Ah. An
image makes you reel, a view of our portly days, of bully bully
boys in wool, swooning in Havana, in Manila. Come. Ride the
wheel once again, high above the pike, where hootchy kootchy
girls tease and barkers beckon yokels to the Streets of Cairo and
the incandescence of progress cancels all notion of night. Spill
toward the floodplain where one day they will bury you, levity
flattened like the prairie into a single horizon.

HOLLY IGLESIAS

Catching the 8:04 to Flee the Heat and the Jesuits

One day at the fair suffices to slake even the idiot's thirst for amusement. I shan't deny that city schools did themselves proud in the mechanical arts, and some of the deaf girls' sewing did show virtuosity. However, the rest was lavish in the extreme, sinful. Fantasy whipped up like a meringue, and to what end? Fifty cents to perspire in the company of strangers.

COLETTE INEZ

Alligator Lunch, Goose Creek

1.

The dog doesn't come back.
Duck feathers float by.
A horse pisses, doves hoo.
They've seen it before
or its likeness.
No comment from the egret
looking for its mate.

Red eyes, a snout's
thrust, the armored body thrashing
through woodlands. I run.

>*Are those shreds of my blue coat,*
>*boot heels spit out on the path?*
>*"She'd just gone for a walk,"*
>*guests tell the police.*

2.

The apple should be quartered
or split for the horse to eat it.
I hold my palm straight out.

>*Is that blood on my palm,*
>*is it my whole hand severed*
>*in the grass?*

I blink.
The mare takes what I offer.
Damp flesh of her nostrils.

I stare into the blood flecked
corners of her half-blind eye—
the alligator basking

through late afternoon, tatters of sky
above the river.

ANNE WARD JAMIESON

From Whitman to Sandburg with Love

From the first yawning
of a single birth
the song of one
small self
a yip a yap a yelp
diminutive affirmative
of this whole nation's
yells and yowls
of its barbaric yawps

to the young yearning
of collective birth
the people yes
clash and blend
yokels yodeling
Yankees yammering
y'all spinnin' yarns
yadda yadda yadda
yeah yeah yeah

TROY JOLLIMORE

How to Get There

You could veer off now, but I think it's best
to keep to the route you've been following
a little while longer. That way you'll have time
to make yourself ready for the eventual departure,
which will inevitably come. Up ahead
you'll find a wide street, full of all sorts of cars,
foreign and domestic. You'll recognize it
by the bright green-red lights that flash at random.
Make a break for the other side.
Swing as far left as you can go—*farther!*—
and drive down that narrow country lane
another twenty or thirty miles. When you get
to the river, the bridge will be out. A dog
will appear as if summoned. This is your sign
to turn back, to look for the tiny side road
that you should have taken before, but could not
because it's only visible once you've passed it.
When you reach the village
(the cluster of white houses)
stop and discard the map.
Also get rid of the passengers.
From here on in they'd only weigh you down.

Leave them by the side of the road. At this point

you'll need a new identity. Call yourself 'Gary.'

Say that you're in 'insurance.'

You'll be due for a maintenance check about now;

use the time to visit the nearby diner

that sells the best cheesecake and worst coffee in the whole

Tri-State area. Flirt with the waitresses.

It might get you slapped but they'll love you for it.

By now you'll have lost too much time; you'll have to

revise destinations. Though in fact

it won't make any difference. Remember,

the laws of physics entail

that the road not taken would have led you to the same place;

or else, it was never accessible at all.

ALLISON JOSEPH

Dazzle

Between the legs, I'm a molten star,
a hot flash of interstellar dust. I'm a
rain-drenched tulip, a dish of lady
fingers, the slap of thigh against thigh,
red innards of a pomegranate. I'm
late-night bordello sweat, the orange
glow of orgasm. I'm Sally Bowles
in the Kit Kat Club, serene as a desert,
granular as a home movie, as snapshots
that behead favorite relatives but still
remain in family albums. I'm a rumpshaker,
baby; if I can't sleep, then you can't either.
No whiter shade of pale for me, no
fragile egg of bliss. I'm ripe as a red
licorice whip snaking around your throat.
"Lucky slut, she's stinky with happiness,"
my friends will covet my blemish-free heart.
I'm a triptych with four parts missing.
Ça plane pour moi when ferns ache
and moss sighs. I'm gravy, gristle,
I'm the plate you lick clean of its grease.

ALLISON JOSEPH

Ms. Jackson Replies

> I'm sorry, Ms. Jackson—I am for real,
> Never meant to make your daughter cry...
>   from "Ms. Jackson," recorded by OutKast

You never meant to make my daughter cry,
but you did. She's wasted too many hours moaning,
sobbing about you and this baby-child, the way

you never come to visit. She blames me for keeping
you away, claims I said you're worthless, shiftless.
I never said no such thing, just that my girl deserves

better than you—with your rapping and jiving,
your music career. I say a career means a man
puts on a coat and tie, speaks correct, knows

English the way it's supposed to be spoken,
not hopping around on stage like someone
on fire. I don't need a roughneck teaching

my grandchild to cuss and drink, to stay up
all hours of the night making music
while respectable men sleep. What kind

of music is that noise anyway—all that silly
rhyming no one can make sense of, just
an excuse for filthy language and a loud beat.

Now if my girl's baby was by Wynton Marsalis,
I wouldn't have a problem—such a fine young
man from a good family with a good education,

so smart they had him on public television
all month. But you, you get on tv and embarrass
me with your so-called apology, saying *you're sorry*

a trillion times. You don't even know
how to count, much less how much
a trillion is. You say you're for real,

but all I see is a phony who raps about hoes
while his child grows up without a proper
role model. You say you're sorry, but not

as sorry as I am that I didn't stop you
from ever seeing, much less touching, my daughter.
You work my last nerve, my last bit of patience,

and I'm not too old to take my belt to you,
let you know how Ms. Jackson gets business done.
But I'm a lady, won't sink to your level.

Just keep sending money, but stay away—
my daughter none of your concern, this
grandchild more like me than you will ever know.

EVE JOSEPH

Four Poems from the Startled Heart

Settle down. Panic, too,
is prayer. A dangerous obsession:

feeding the stars by fire,
and nobody to tell.

In the garden, a ghost, unconcerned,
working the soil.

Such beauty in the flawed: sitting down
to the evening meal. Pass the potatoes, please.

I do not see what he sees. A blank canvas:
his mind on it. A line of fire.

If a radif, then let it be mercy.
Singed by fear: a near miss. Dear God, mercy.

EVE JOSEPH

What we hold of fire
in our hands: ashes, burnt words,

a cracked plate: a boy
on the other side, licking it clean.

The smell of smoke: a fistful
of lily of the valley. The wrought

iron gate keeps nobody out.
Delicate black vines and grapes.

I cook crepes for my brother,
thirty years later:

feed him in death
as I never could in life.

EVE JOSEPH

A starling with no feet
eats at my table: a few crumbs, dried cranberries.

Where does it get me,
my foolish pity?

Intentional or not, you stepped
in death's way.

A bone-white edge, the near perfect
fit of broken things.

Too late for lessons now. A blackbird spoke
because you asked.

It's hope that does me in: the place
the voice breaks.

What's left? A kind of grace:
a perilous landing.

EVE JOSEPH

Against such blue skies, the crow
finds nowhere to hide.

In my death poem, light will find me
defiant and unprepared.

I'll write a letter to each of my children;
I'll steal what I must: white fields

and a man writing himself off
to God.

The mind returns
to the last place, finds

the river is, after all
only a river.

Ravens fly straight, not crows:
tell me, which way will I go?

JESSE LEE KERCHEVAL

God has no name.

My great grandmother had many
but no one knows them now.

My name is Jesse. I write this to remember.

My mother's name was Olive,
her mother's name was Ethel.

Will I live long enough—I wonder—
to see Ethel back in style?

My mother also had a cousin Cumi—*Talitha Cumi*,
Jesus said & raised her from the dead.

The devil, fallen angel, has such pretty names—
(Satan so like satin) but then he

is not God.

God has no name. What will I call him

when he comes?

JESSE LEE KERCHEVAL

I Want To Tell You

I heard Joyce Carol Oates say writing
was like pushing a pea   across a warehouse with your nose
you crawl crawl crawl along
& when you look up—
dirty floorboards as far as you can see stretching   to forever.
I think she was talking about a novel.
I think she was talking about *Blonde*
a novel she was writing about Marilyn Monroe.
I am talking about this poem.
Pea & no princess, nose in the dirt
pushing pushing pushing & so little progress.
I am talking about poetry.
I am talking about breaking out of the neat little box of
     humorous lines
rising to a   *zing*
of cosmic meaning at the end.
I know—I've written them too.   Still do--
poems too damn much like Methodist sermons.
First the joke about little Johnny & God
(Johnny thinks the hymn "Bringing the Sheaves" is "Bringing in
     The Sheets!"—
I always thought it was "Bringing in the Sheep"—
Oh well guess I'm damned).
Then the metaphor about how the minister's windshield wipers
not working in a terrible rain storm
is like trying to fathom
The Will of God
(in both cases you have no idea where you are going).
A quick reference to scripture   & pass the plate.
What about everything this sermon/ my poem has left unsaid?
About how we are dying all dying   how people I love
     are already dead?

(no stanza break)

180

this year   my sister-in-law
sixteen years ago in April   my mom
eighteen years Tuesday   my dad
in a day or a decade   me   & you too   don't
    kid yourself
My daughter told me she doesn't want to die or get married
Some days I know just what she means
Now in the other room I hear her & two friends who spent the
night singing
LoveLoveLoveLoveLove   *Makes the World Go Round*
My daughter who turned 12 last night—New Year's Eve—
& we all stood on the frozen grass of the Capitol square
watching fireworks   explode off   the glass bank across
    the street
Glad that's not our bank my husband said
when he saw the firemen poised   hoses at the ready
Hey just like 'Nam he added as a joke though he would know
Each concussion   a fist   in the chest
Each burst red/green/gold sizzling twisting
stars falling out of the universe & into our eyes
I start to laugh & I start to cry
& even   at the end of this poem
I have no earthly idea why

ROBERT KING

Report

I have visited the houses we left behind,
found the scrawny cedar we endured
removed, the porch deftly repaired

or not, the fences replaced or taken down,
the color a surprise, perhaps, but they
seem generally stronger, prettier.

The houses that held us in for years
have, most of them, stayed married.
They have gone on with their lives.

ROBERT KING

Impediment

The man at the nearby table
laboriously forces his talk,
muscling his chest to grunt,
resting after each word.
I try to hear what's worth this.

Only a fragile story, but he wants
to tell it, no matter the effort,
and lifts another syllable
into its place, a monument
to ordinary life, language poised
in air, each day this miracle.

KARI LYNNE KINKELE

a bastard of Poseidon

my mother lives in me
as blue crashes white foam against my atmosphere.
gray mother, blue daughter
her echo near reverb
like the space inside a seashell
held to a wanting ear.
i find myself speaking her words in my voice
but the meaning is drown in the tide.
my arms flail her gestures.
thoughts scuttle like crabs
then bury themselves under a hard shell.
i am sitting at the place where push and pull meet
waves overlap each other
one rolls, another recedes

the rule of the undertow

DAVID KIRBY

Massimo's Secret Rome

All summer long we'd been looking forward
    to staying at the Senato,
because for years Massimo had told us if we'd just stay
    a little longer, he'd show us
Massimo's secret Rome, the one the tourists never see,
    but when we get there,
first the others say Massimo will be back August 1,
    then August 15, and then they say

he won't be back at all, that he's gone to another hotel,
    and finally they say he's been
hired away at a much better salary and would we please
    not tell anyone because
Massimo had been so popular with the clients,
    had brought in so much
business, now they are afraid the old clients won't come
    any more, will go to

Massimo's new hotel or maybe just any hotel, because
    what is the Senato now,
they say, without Massimo? But without Massimo,
    we say, what is Rome?
All we can do is say, what is Massimo's secret Rome?
    It certainly wouldn't be
Paris, which is a waiter sweeping out a café,
    lovers coming home

at dawn, a grandma watching a child sail a boat
    on a pond,
a poodle shivering from the cold. Nor would it be Munich,
    which is a ceramic beer stein,

(no stanza break)

a diva wearing a horned helmet, and the word *nicht*
    canceling everything
that precedes it. And it wouldn't be London,
    which is exquisite manners,

a Cockney accent, tea sandwiches with the crusts cut off,
    driving on the wrong side,
a guitarist who plays like an angel but is missing a tooth.
    Or even Florence,
which is a glass of sangiovese, Michelangelo's *David*,
    fresh leather first thing
in the morning, a kid showing you a newspaper
    while another picks your pocket.

No, we'll have to find our own secret Rome,
    and Cesare Pavese
and Giacomo Leopardi will be in it,
    but so will Little Richard
and Walt Whitman as well. There'll be a meal:
    salmon and anchovies
with a glass of flinty white wine, then a piece
    of roasted cheese

drizzled with honey and a coarse red wine, then melon
    and figs and a dessert wine.
And bread throughout, good bread. There'll be cute dogs,
    like corgis and
Jack Russell terriers. There'll be an opera with a duke,
    a traitor, a castle, a dwarf,
a mud hat, a river made of cardboard waves, lots of swords,
    and two elixirs,

one poisoned and one not. There'll be movies:
    we'll see Vittorio De Sica's
Ladri di Biciclette and Frederico Fellini's *Roma*
    but also Michael Tolkin's *Rapture*
and John Sayles's *Matewan*, and when they are over,
    as we leave the theater,
we'll blink in the sunlight and move slowly, like dreamers
    waking after a long sleep.

And everything will look nice in this secret city of ours,
        this city-within-a-city,
but it'll look weird, too, and trapezoidal, the buildings starting out
        the size of shoeboxes as they
burst from the pavement but then flaring wildly as they soar
  skyward
        and turn different colors
and bang against each other and make loud musical clangs

        rather than the crunching
or grinding noises you'd expect buildings to make as they collide.
        And we'll be rich
and also immortal because we'll have all the words we'll ever
  need--
        billions of dollars
worth of words will fly down the streets continuously,
        and nobody will know it but us!
Well, also Mr. Pavese and Mr. Leopardi and Mr. Richard
        and Mr. Whitman—they'll know.

For your flummery and claptrap and fiddle-faddle,
        your twiddle-twaddle
and gibble-gabble and rantum-scantum
        and skimble-skamble,
why, even your flummadiddle, your falderal, your flubdub:
        reader, surely these are
the 10- and 20-dollar bills of our language! And their equal
        in liras to boot.

Then, on the day we are leaving, as we are putting
        our luggage into the taxi
at seven o'clock in the morning, for heaven's sake,
        and struggling to load not only
everything we brought with us but also our new acquisitions,
        almost all of which are either
breakable or oddly shaped or both, what do we hear
        but a familiar voice:

"Hello, friends!" It's Massimo! And he embraces us
        and apologizes for not
meeting us and tells us about his new job but quickly,
        because we have to go,
and he says we must come see him next time we're in town,
        and then he'll show us
a side of the city we've never seen before, he'll show us
        "Massimo's secret Rome."

DAVID KIRBY

Mr. Dithers Explains It All to You

Friend tells me *her* friend kept an amp
    in the trunk of their car so they could get into shows,
elbowing the doorman aside with an "Excuse me,
        excuse me, damn it!" and no one saying a thing,
because who'd go to all that trouble
    if they weren't part of the entertainment?

As it says on the wall of every dry cleaner's in America,
    there's no substitute for hard work.
A writer might say, as Gide did, "I rewrite in order
        to be reread." Or he might echo
Thomas Mann and say, "A writer is someone for whom writing
    is more difficult than it is for other people."

Or he might open the paper and read "Dagwood": in today's
    episode,
        Mr. Dithers is saying, "Bumstead! Why haven't you
started on that report to the stockholders?!"
        and Dagwood replies, "I'm waiting for inspiration
to strike," but then he's flying through the air,
    and now he's at his computer: "Dear Stockholders...."

And look at him—he doesn't even have a hair
    out of place! Ol' Dag is bowed but he isn't bloody;
he is the buck private of his soul. Later, he will have
        a big sandwich and a long nap while Daisy lies
alongside the sofa adoringly, waiting for him to wake,
    but right now he's got that report to write.

Maybe "Dagwood" should be on the dry cleaner's wall.
    The Hasidim have a tale about a rabbi named Meir

(no stanza break)

189

who used to worry that God would reproach him
                in his final days and say, "Meir! Why did you not
become Meir?" Here's a formula for you:
      1 Dagwood + 1 Mr. Dithers = 1 Meir.

Notice it's always "Mr. Dithers," by the way,
      and never "Julius," whereas it's either "Dagwood"
or "Bumstead" and never "Mr. Bumstead."
          But amps—I've never lifted one—are really heavy,
    aren't they?
Didn't Ginger Rogers say she had to do everything
      Fred Astaire did, only backwards and in heels?

SHERRYL KLEINMAN

In the Body

Pain crosses state lines
with a minor,
staying in motels
with orange shag,
one bulb,
a toilet flushing slow.

He gets tired of one place,
moves on, leaving behind
something: a battered suitcase,
worn shoes, rusty corkscrew.

The thirteen year-old is glum.
She's tired of moving,
every room the same but each
bed bunches in a different place.

Just when she learns exactly
where to put each leg
it's time to move on.
Down another highway.
Maybe the same highway.

He doesn't want her to know.
She might learn something,
get confident, run away.
She thinks there's nowhere to run.

The world is a Motel 6
squatting on asphalt next to a diner.
Another waitress in beige pours coffee
into a white cup with a green band.

He lets her read comics, but they bore her.
Sometimes he talks about himself.
He used to carve holsters
for the details, the smell of leather.

He never touches her.
He knows that soon
she'll take his hand.

TED KOOSER

Best Face

"Just put on your best face," Mother would say,
telling me how to get on in the world,
and I've knotted its straps so many mornings
that I'm used to the heat, the stickiness,
the intractable stiffness around the mouth.

The fabric's worn thin, with a few small patches,
and it's spotted with stains, and today
at the mirror I could almost see through it
into that other face, the one I started with
so many years ago, not the best face
but my own small fearful kisser, peering out,
hoping for someone to show it the way.

TED KOOSER

Closing the Windows

First, the uncertain white fingers
of lightning, fumbling around
with the black hem of the county,
peering in under, then thunder,
then the flat slap of the first drop
on the roof, like a fingertip
tapping, "Right here, put the rain
here." And then my father
in his summer pajamas
moving in silhouette, closing
the windows, no word from he
who swept through the house
like flashing shadow, but a chatter
of leaves blown over the shingles,
the clunk of sash weights
deep in the walls, then the storm
muffled by spattered glass.
It was all so ordinary then
to see him at the foot of the bed,
closing a squeaky window,
but more than fifty years have passed
and now I understand that it was
not so ordinary, after all.

TED KOOSER

A Jar of Buttons

This is a core sample
from the floor of the Sea of Mending,

a cylinder packed with shells
that over many years

sank through fathoms of shirts—
pearl buttons, blue buttons—

and settled together
beneath the waves of perseverance,

an ocean upon which
generations of women set forth,

under the sails of gingham curtains,
and seated side by side

on decks sometimes salted by tears,
made small but important repairs.

RAPHAEL KOSEK

Mary Todd Lincoln

I don't know how he lived with her,
she, with him. The sweet round face
bred to be happy, a full, pleasant life—
not the deep worry of a tall, thin man
who was friend to insomnia,
who weighed the light and the dark,
who deviled himself with the broken country.

How could they not drink the water
of the Potomac? lose a son
to the malaria tainted airs of a city
surrounded by swamp?
the unspeakable sacrifice Abraham nearly made,
more real than any happiness
they ever knew, old hands at losing sons.

How to leave such losses, cut short mourning,
carry the weight? – serious responsibility
must consecrate such a one as he,
but she, with her soft full body,
her smiling into occasional madness,

some said, childishness, the spendthrift ways
as if three hundred pairs of lace gloves
could buy back what grief swallowed,
a vase here, a rich cushion there,
to soften the bare walls,
the rough hewn face that bore the brunt.

She couldn't bear to attend the funeral.

How could she not be forgiven?

(no stanza break)

196

Even falling into debt can have its blessings.
And madness, after all, is a haven of sorts
not far from heaven.

DAVID KRESH

Homage to Raphael Soyer

The passerby pass by in bright
rags and flesh.
I stand at the gate
watchful.

There were woods in the city,
patient, knobby, blindered horses
drawing wagons with clanking
ropes of bells,
parrots and monkeys on gypsies' shoulders.
Brown photos smelling of vinegar.

My earliest memory: the doctor
brought me in his satchel
and I heard my brother
walking around in the kitchen.

Squirrels zigzag in the bare branches.
The park benches are full,
old men with turned up overcoat collars,
fedoras with dully shiny bands,
smell of Luckies and Wings thick
in their moustaches, haggles and mutters of
liquid Yiddish, they spit in disdain,
they sit patient, they look in the air.
Spring is coming.

Who knew in those days
riding the el uptown,
everywhere there are Jews,
the parents speaking,
not Yiddish, Russian,
the children shouldn't understand.

Oh! one thinks when
one is young, to
be invisible!
unknown! when one
is.

Brown photos:
trim and straight,
thick curled moustache
and bright liquid oriental eye.
Vest and watch chain.
Firm hand on the back of a chair.
The Montenegran bandit!

Brown photos:
high-bosomed round-cheeked
young woman, ringlets
and ribbon at her throat,
locket and frills,
pretty and proud before
we children came.

Who knew, the children
everywhere, and Papa
where? drinking with the card players.
And the oldest, the curious one,
goes in Papa's shoe store
and takes one of the knives
and cuts open her hand.

Long ago once
walking in my neighborhood
--I remember it was Easter—
I became jaunty, I sauntered
with hands in pockets.
I passed a yard where a smaller boy
picked up stones and slowly
threw them at me.

(no stanza break)

I'll call my sister! he said.
She came out, smirking and big.
Not running, walking
quickly, yes, but not running.

Who knew, if you asked
Mama always said
when you grow up
you'll know and understand.

The tunnel smells of the dust
of cement and yellow paper.
At the end is
the bright square of the areaway.
Sweet old country
fiddling, singing
for flung-down pennies,
housewives in housedresses,
bosoms on sills, lean
above the laundry,
tears in their eyes,
pennies floating down through
flapping sheets and pigeons.

In the mosaic stairwell splashed
through a filmy window with
walk-up sun, an older boy
called Bernie The Hammer says
do you believe in God?
You shouldn't believe in God,
you should believe in the sun.
It gives the energy.
It makes everything grow.
It makes it so you could
see. Without the sun
what would there be?
Nothing!

The light drawn
up into the eyes.

An etching press
you could get for $25.
We didn't use fancy paper.
We used what we had.

We could go out together
like Gauguin and van Gogh
and stand in the middle of the street
and paint. There was still
space in the city.
There was still perspective.

Who knew, cocky
with cap and Caporal in
squinted lips, left eye
shadowed by smoke
watchful at the mirror.

"Young people...they have
nothing to lose.
They must begin somewhere."

"We were young and had fun."

At the Art Center
the small proud old men
waiting to judge,
to welcome.

Who knew, the slim
marcelled steno lighting
a Murad pursed in
bright rose lips
hurrying to meet her friends
the artists at Romany Marie's.

(*no stanza break*)

She pauses to adjust
her stocking, drawing her
skirt up to her knee.

In those days models wore
many underclothes and their
gestures of dressing and undressing
were complex, interesting, and explanatory.

"Time had a different
property then—there
seemed so much of it."

On gray days
the perspective was clear,
giving a sense of space
and loneliness unbroken
by shadows.

A professor of art history once told me
that Rembrandt loved to stroll through the
Jewish quarter observing "the sadness
of Jewish features in repose." Obligingly,
I reposed my features, why not?

Hands make small natural
gestures of their own:
thumb gripped inside first finger
and the delicate little finger extended,
slight turning forward of the palm,
pushing up the cheek,
clasped under the pregnant belly,
resting lightly on a cane.

When one is young, it's fun,
everything is opening to the eye,
you do something, it's better
than what you did before.
Later, there is more doubt
and stubbornness.

What do you have
to work with? Only
everything in the world that you can see.
Only yourself.

"Look at it long, study it.
Who knows if you will
ever see it again."

My sister was
the first of us
to die.

She sits round in the flesh
looking up with blotted blue eyes,
looselaced shoes, knuckles
clasped in her lap.
The piano is shut
in the corner.
Who once was so
slender, brilliant and dancing.

I talked with the German salesman
in the seat beside me.
When the train stopped at Oswiecim
the embankment was splashed with wildflowers.
The German traveller was also
moved by their beauty.
"Of course" he smiled at me
"Auschwitz is famous for its flowers."

Every day more
I shrug myself into
the warm worn hand-me-down
of my father's gestures.
I stare into his face
in my mirror.

Open your eyes, haunted
windows where the dead
can sometimes be seen
moving behind the curtain.

Some names I've forgotten.

"That was a long time ago."

"Today I would have simplified this a lot."

"I could have simplified it,
but that's the way it is."

"I'm a witness, and I look a little
confused because I *am* confused."

The passersby pass by, and years,
in the streets always young
women as sure as flowers.

Gypsy, a dancer, often
comes to my studio.
Today she says "Today
I'll tell your fortune."
She strokes the lines of my palm
with electric attention
--like being looked at by Dürer—
I have confidence in her.
She still holds my hand
and looks sadly and
lovingly into my eyes.
"I think I won't tell you
your fortune." There pops into
my head the phrase "life and works."

When I look up from my work
it is already light and late

(*no stanza break*)

October. I have formed the letters
across the stone which say
"Know Thy Self." I look out
with loose empty hands
and eyebrows raised in surprise.
"A man has how many faces."

Craning over a passing shoulder
I form the glyphic
gesture that might mean
hello, or goodbye
or maybe some sort of blessing
or merely here, here I am.

"It was not meant to convey
anything in particular."

MAXINE KUMIN

Eating Babies

Think of setting sail from Tollesbury in Essex
for Sydney, Australia in 1884.
You'd have to bully your way around Cape Horn
where 200 days a year the sea heaves up gale storms
known as the willawaws, thrusting you, mere specks
into God's hard hands from a yacht named the Mignonette.

A thousand miles from any land mass, you are swamped.
The yacht goes down in an instant to Davy Jones.
Barely time to scramble aboard the bare-bones
dinghy without any water or food except
for two tins of turnips you learn to love. Adrift
on day four you catch a small turtle. Nothing else floats by.

You are Dudley and Stephens and Brooks and skinny, shy
young Parker, your cabin boy, who, on the fifteenth day
gulps quantities of seawater to slake his thirst
and soon thereafter lies delirious, then comatose.
On the twentieth day two of you decide
that unless one is killed, all four of you will die.

You, Dudley and you, Stephens slit the cabin boy's throat
(Brooks dissents and does not participate)
and all three of you feed from his body and blood
for the next four days. Then you are rescued.
You are honor-bound to divulge what you have done.
After all, you are Englishmen, you serve the Crown.

Is this *Homicide founded on Necessity?*
You *put to death a weak and unoffending boy.*
Whether this be or be not murder the Court must say.

(no stanza break)

206

You, Dudley and you, Stephens are ordered to be hanged
but the Queen commutes your sentence to six months'
imprisonment, which you serve out gallantly.

Brooks gets off (it seems, although accounts vary, scot-free).
To preserve one's life is generally speaking a duty,
the Crown pronounced. *But it may be the plainest
and highest duty to sacrifice it.* Amen,
but is it one's highest duty on the high seas
to starve to death a thousand miles from land?

Examples abound: among the Aztec
history tells us, the c-word was an ecological necessity.
On Easter Island, man was the only large mammal
available. It wasn't so long ago that tribesmen
cooked and devoured two Peruvian traders.
In the pits of the Anasazi, in the Southwest

anthropologists have found bits of human flesh
in human feces. The Japanese are said to
have eaten P.O.W.'s during World War II
and the starving Chinese—this may be a canard—
are reputed to supplement their impoverished diets
with fetuses. Shades of Dean Jonathan Swift!

Let us not overlook our very own Donner Party
whether they did or didn't. (They did.) But are we
to view cannibalism as always in extremis?
More than one tribe ate human flesh unapologetically;
fingers and toes were considered the choicest morsels.
What do we in the First World know of unappeasable hunger?

It's easy to satisfy lust, we eat, as we say, like pigs
greasy gourmands at the chain-food restaurants.
We're guilty of feeding chopped-up cattle parts
to fatten cattle for slaughter, and other acts
that go against nature. But what happens if we persist?
What if the environment so degrades that it can

no longer sustain the products we ask it to yield?
What if the water's not fit to drink, the sour fields
go sterile—sick steer, poisoned lambs, infertile hens
drive us to eating pigeons and rats, as in
Amsterdam, 1945? Then on to
killing and eating each other, like the Anasazi?

Imagine a time not far from our own:
we are the last species left that is able to breed
and eight out of ten of us now is born
with shrivelled lungs, a lollipop brain stem.
If you didn't know what you were eating at first
wouldn't your hungers drive you to taste?

Baby tongue, a delicious hors d'oeuvre, baby heart
lightly sauteed in baby fat, a substitute
for the now-vanished olive oil. Roast loin of baby...
And the famed law-school case of *Regina
v. Dudley and Stephens and Brooks* will be
viewed as a quaint misstep, ancient legal history.

MAXINE KUMIN

Historic Blacksburg, Virginia

The lavatory sign still reads
Colored on one side and White
on the other in the old
caboose that used to trail
the ravelled skein of freight cars full
of West Virginia coal.
Whoever entered had to flip
his designation right side up
then brace against the track before
unbuttoning, back to the door
and pissing down the same foul hole.

DANIEL J. LANGTON

Soldiering

A gun on either side of me, a pond
with blood and foam, shit and corpses in it;
among the lily's pads, empty boxes
of bullets, bandages and processed food;
a quiet made up of too much blatant sound,
grass and weeds smashed by up-to-the-minute
shards of metal riven to find the fox's
hole I dug to do some transient good.

It is morning in her bedroom, soon she'll
dress and wander to her coffee, safe as sun,
while I huddle beneath a canopy
of shells, not sea shells, not the bursting shells
of peas, just chunks of murder left undone.
War is mere death, love made a man of me.

DANIEL J. LANGTON

With Her in an Urban Forest

The dense insistence of crows,
conversations on a train
in China, the darkened trees
looking ready to take fright,
the din, as far as that goes,
as real on our skin as rain
or the skittish legs of bees
out for the first time at night.
Then it was still, and all those
branches burdened with the strain
of silence bowed like Chinese
on the train, in calm delight.
"Eve," (before the moment flew)
"they all stopped to look at you."

DANIEL J. LANGTON

Weddings & Births, Births & Weddings

I was in the greeting card section of the store
and all around me people were reading verse,
measured passion, rimed love, graduation—
cheap wine and cheap music at the party too—
but there they were, Poetry, there they were,
imagining poems as they imagine Paris,
surprised there is such a place, as though fantasies
could have side streets, traffic lights, fatigue;
touching words like ecstacy and esperanza,
fingering the Pieta, and I remembered Mays
and the beer man yelling "Poetry in motion"
as Ginsberg smiled. Lines and forces.
A tender weakened homage to the longed for,
the glimpsed, the just missed, the puzzling echo.

DANIEL J. LANGTON

The Thaw

The earth is solid, solid for once.
There is light and there is darkness,
they make no difference, it all defines
itself in stillness. Nothing will give in;
the rabbits in the snow, the fish
beneath the ice, are not part of it,
though they point it out, they point it out.

The living things are sensible,
the living things are frightened.
The first sound an emphatic crack,
the race has started, the glacier
will reveal it is water, the stone
that it is stone; the cold recedes,
an embarrassed lover; worms turn.

Quiet is quiet, the bear's dream needs quiet,
its fleas don't dream. When sleep is over,
heads rise like suns, the blunt moles
move upward, as the daisies will, at will.

(no stanza break)

The light stays longer and longer,

colors get mixed; corpses, rigid and dumb,

soften to feed what is to be fed.

Sounds make movements, movements make sounds.

Tails swish, throats grumble, the tense air

becomes hospitable, the birds will arrive,

regret the silence, cry out against silence,

needing each other, needing the songs.

Smells will happen, noses will flare,

the play resume with a different cast.

LOY LEDBETTER

Breakfast at the Ritz

I am having breakfast at the Ritz
but I don't wear my jewelry.
He didn't tell me where we were going
so I wear my orange pants
with the petunias spread across the butt,
tennis shoes in yellow and Partytime Pink,
an orange T-shirt, tight but plain
with only my rhinestone, rabbit, lapel pin.
I don't want to look too conspicuous.

I could have worn my heart-shaped zircon
and flashed it around like the woman
at the window table with her rock.
She is flashy; teased top, cinched bottom,
gold bangles mold her wrist and neck.
Watching her reminds me of the old saw,
        Do you know how chorus girls get mink?
        Probably, the same way mink get mink.

That blue lady—hat, hair, dress, shoes—
squints at me along her nose. Ha!
Twenty years ago when she
went out to eat, she ate at a diner.
I might be Queen of Sheba later on.

Those ladies in the corner spot
with their Nieman suits and Gucci shoes
have class. They only look at me
with sidelong glances.

I guess I'll give them all another show
and parade back to the 'buffit' for seconds.
I feel the need to feed my petunias.

GARY LEISING

A Pedestrian Poem

To the woman at the bus stop
I am the cartoon coyote, frozen,
a foot hangs above the pavement: *Homo Pedestrian*,
the everyday, undistinguished man, bold,
democratic, the way Whitman must have felt
as he wandered through shipyards or passed
escaped slaves on a long dirt road. My steps
could come from *Leaves of Grass*
or Dickinson's poem about hope.

Cars keep coming, ignore the crosswalk sign,
its yellow light, a sun not noticed doing
what it does. *You're keeping this poor man
from work*, my expression says. One car stops,
traffic in the other direction continues, and I
stand on the twin yellow lines, narrow
my waist, following a Pilates instructor's words,
*Stand straight as if there's a harness on your head
pulling it to the ceiling as you inhale.* I stretch,
afraid of exhaling as side mirrors slip by,
their plastic backs, hip-high, the color of bruises.

The worst cars rush by: the bumper of a Civic
wants to break my legs, an SUV could flatten me,
a Camaro—its chrome-plated dual exhausts shine
like ceremonial daggers—longs for my body
outlined on its hood. Then, some hope,
a block away, a station wagon, its driver
a mother of four grown children. She'll see me,
think of the son she loves the most, the one
who didn't finish college and can't hold
a steady job. She'll stop.

RODNEY TERICH LEONARD

Vodka Sunday

Four young girls and a baby brother
trace the woods
by mercy of the moon.

Granddaddy chased them away
cocking his gun.
Briar-torn legs bled a simpler truth:
No enjoying June today.

Ever smiled an alcoholic
into burying his bully?
Probably easier to patty cake with the sun.

DANIEL H. LIGHTSEY

Between Sets

The August fog rolled down Broadway in balls,
Like bramble-bushes in a black and white western;
Past Mike's Pool Hall
Where sharks ran cracking nine-ball racks.
There, sitting on a stool professorial, was John Birks Gillespie,
Cooling the inner-walls of his caterwauling chops;
Contemplating the demise of bop,
And the rise of Jimi Hendrix, and Janis Joplin,
Arcing electric to sell-out crowds at Winterland.
While, in a wood shed in New Orleans,
Wynton Marsalis was cutting his.
But then, great poems rarely play to packed houses.

ELLINE LIPKIN

Cosmetics

(fr. *kosmein* to arrange, fr. *kosmos* order)

Violet Rain, Violent Rain.
At the cosmetics company
I mis-type eyeshadow labels
testers will wear in the city.
Violent Rain seems appropriate
for something close to the eye
I decide, and say nothing.

From the 47th floor
the skyscraped sky
bruises from Teal Haze
into Almost Black.
The late-lit office windows
brighten into beads of light,
squares of amber necklaced
across the city's string of
late-day deadlines and ambition.
Night's dusk-colored camisole
fades against a chair,
waiting to be put on.

Leaning against the glass wall,
I see Manhattan's grid flatten
into a black net skirt
a careening ambulance rips
straight down the back.
At each stoplight streaks
of Taxi Yellow blur against
the sidewalk's sloppy gloss,
Pavement Pallor blended
with All-Day Soot, sheened

(no stanza break)

219

with overturned trash cans,
blue undertones of psychotic fit,
and iridescent glints of rage.
The buildings press themselves
against each rouge-smear
of grease and tallow while again
the train rapes the tunnel.

I fight vertigo and lean
into the glass, my body hovering
into the city's moving silhouette.
My face presses against
its neon fire, its limn of steely rail
lining my eyes as they mirror
Subway Dun, Exhaustion Blanche,
Yearning's Silver Kohl.

DUANE LOCKE

At the River Styx

The ferryman is now unemployed,
Spends all day
Watching talk shows on television.
He is no longer needed by the dead;
For now the dead in bikinis
Swim over on their own.
The river waters are speckled
With their lost dark glasses.
There are so many dead,
Such an overpopulation,
That at the crematory,
The dead have to stand in long lines.
As the dead wait,
The dead are served crème de menthe.
Sometimes it takes years
Before the dead are cremated.
The people who loved the dead
When the dead were alive
Are found sitting
With empty urns
In their living rooms.

GEORGE LOONEY

One Definition of Chance

Slow and given to tantrums, the boy who counts
ghosts, thwapping each on the head,
never has gotten the swing of numbers,

every statistic he collects suspect. Dead on
or not, there is no way to verify,
independently, his count. Everyone

gives him a wide berth, and has for years,
his discussions with himself infamous
for miles, the fever of his hands in the air

while he speaks legend and off-putting. Drunks
use the numbers he gives them to play
the daily lotto. The corner preacher hears them

as chapter and verse for the day's sermon.
Chance, the preacher says, is just one way
to define the Lord's hand in everything,

the slow boy just one of His servants.
The slow boy keeps counting. Every day,
the dead line up to listen to the sour rantings

of the preacher. Thwap, thwap, the slow boy
counts, the dead rising, pale butterfly koi,
to the fever of his hand on their foreheads

as though each thwap is the blessing they've been
waiting for since long before they entered
this murky world. How easy it is to be lost.

A. LOUDERMILK

Married Women: a Sideshow

500 bolts off-white, my bride. With all
that gas in her belly, she rumbled
like a kicked bee box. Titanic lady,
she left me, too big for her legs,
too buxom to vacuum. So pretty
in the face. I loved her. Everyone
laughed. Hippopotamus. I loved you.

> *(2 Women: Alice the house all premature
> grey & Berl the smoker, horse-dentured
> or toothless. Each a punchline. Everyone
> knew. The big lady's dead now & Berl she
> mows yards in summer, cleans out gutters
> May & November. Every spring a poem
> for A's birthday from B
> w/ love on the last page of the Gazette.)*

Barn-woman, my housewife. With all
those streamlining tricks: she crossed
her arms downward to bully her gut
& feature her wrists, actually so
delicate. House-slippered mama,
everyone stared. Your heart said stop
& they cut you open. Polished honey
flowed from my sweetheart. Sugarhips.
Tubaist. Star of my barge & railroad car.

ALICE LYONS

The Plural of Rome

So many house of God here
so much old adoration
so much beseeching.
The air's thick with prayers
already said
spent vespers, used-up alleluias
ancient oxygen.
Ages of Ave Marias bivouac
on the doorsteps of your ears
and murmur and murmur…

Breathe in in Rome
your lungs are bivalve
churches—packed, temporary, airy
lacking in particulars.

I prayed in two, both Mary ones
the mother of God God enough
you'd imagine.
Sent up my deepest longing
tossed it up with the gazillion
and lit white candles
--part lardy matter
part captured weather—
to represent my heart's incarnate state.
In Rome, in the din, amid the many
I asked God to speak my very name.

ALICE LYONS

Reunion

Out of the booze and dope-soaked West Belfast
you walked intact
marked with an interrogative regard
a Northern weather-eye
that inquires more than it declares a guard
not to be let down.

With your firecracker lexicon of fer fuck's sakes
and soda farls
verbs declining like the Springfield Road
do, done, done—
not even you could dodge that community tattoo:
trust no one.

(My Yankee ingenuity and knowhow
sought you out
thought I could undo the Ballymurphy in you
I could not.)

So I walked, licked wounds, threw a few
bricks.

Then a greening—no a graying
something amid black and white
it brought you back.

You lifted her, our daughter
saying *Tell Mommy everything you seen*

And I saw a Saracen turned inside out
I saw

(no stanza break)

the rivets and steel of your strong frame
I saw
your soft soul
forged in an overturned bus, aflame.

ELIZABETH MARSH

Beyond Gender

Two girls and two guys
No—three girls, one guy
Two girls, one guy
And a baseball hat with baggy clothes

A young face
Mounds that fill a sweatshirt
Yet, pinstriped boxers
What about the hair?

Then the words:
Childlike and playful

Finally a name
Maggie became an identity

TRAPETA B. MAYSON

You Are 12

You are 12 and your mother is crazy.
You don't know what it all means but you scared.
You hear her answering herself, you see
her shaving her head bald and drawing blood.
You feel her moving in the night while you
hold your breath in the dark. She different now.
She mean and you believe that she hates you.
It's bad enough you dark and African,
nappy and flat chested in the 80's.
Now yall the neighborhood joke, not quite as
bad as Poo and them whose father killed his
own brother over pork chops one Sunday.
But yall up there / top of the line misfits.
It's a small block and yall are too well known.
They whisper about your family and
they greet the police cars weekly after
her latest outburst. Philadelphia's
finest drag your crazy mama somewhere
looking like a big ripped up old rag doll.
Their eyes say they sorry for you but you
know better. They are satisfied. *Yeah them
uppity African niggas who thought
they was so much better done fell on they
face.* You lose your father to shame and your
brother to the streets. Your sisters become
your children. Problems weigh your ass way down.
You the woman of the house. You are 12.

TRAPETA B. MAYSON

By the Roadside
For Liberian survivors of war

The girl who used to plait my hair
had fingers like vines   tough and elegant.
She parted and divided me with those hands,
guiding my head between her thighs—
inviting me into a world of dark spices.

I imagined some young boy planting himself
within the folds of her lapa—
her shining eyes encouraging him to delve deep.

She was our good witch, our hair sorcerer.
I waited at her alter to be anointed,
taking my turn between warm knees,
believing in her powers to consecrate me.

So when they cut off those hands
and left her on Gbarnga Road,
I wondered how they knew
to take that part of her—
Those vines,
those lovely, lovely vines,
that once turned
plain country women
into goddesses.

KATHLEEN McGOOKEY

During the Day

I invite my dreams to come to me. At first, nothing. I hadn't realized
   they were shy.
Then the doorbell rings and I see puffs of dust rise under the dream's
   invisible feet, which
are running away.

They send me an Australian shepherd in the midst of a thunderstorm.
   She is scared but
polite, and begs to come into the house. But she has a collar; she
   belongs elsewhere; I send
her back into the rain. She sits and delicately raises one paw: she doesn't
   want to disobey
them, or me.

I buy a glass door and leave it open. I put a pool table in the living
   room and bring in
many comfortable chairs. I kick the mice out of my dishes. The dreams
   send word that
only the bad eggs are coming. They want to smoke in the house. Soon
   I'm falling off
cliffs in my own backyard, in broad daylight, scribbling my last words on
   goldfish which
float like petals into the sky.

My dreams deliver charred bacon, a deep pit. Velvet that crumbles and
   alligators loosed in
the streets. Empty picture frames, the gold leaf chipped, festooned
   with damp tendrils of
seaweed. A half-empty jar of salsa: they call it *portable sunset*.

They know I'm at their mercy. Still, I ask for my first dead friend's lost
   philosophy
book. Plato. Hours later, I find only the title page in my dog's mouth,
   partly shedded
but still recognizable, her name scribbled on it, faintly, in pen.

RENNIE McQUILKIN

On Assignment in Uganda

I focus my lens on the boy's upper lip
with its curve and cleft of love's bow
strung with a sweet line of lower lip.

He has turned from the broken wall of
a smouldering church, has taken in what
my camera has shot—hundreds

locked inside, charred piles of bone
sparkling with shards of stained glass.
He knew them,

holds a sprig of rosemary
to breathe through, sweeten the stench.
It doesn't

keep his lower lip from trembling,
tightening, pulling away from the bow,
no longer love's, beginning

to release a scream. Let it be shrill
enough to shatter the lens
I see through.

PETER MEINKE

The Deserted Village, 2002

Even the best villages are deserted
by someone their abandoned windows staring
like lonely women who have done everything
right all they were taught to do yet find themselves
at the end of life curled below a dark hill
with night drifting in and the cry of a barred
owl the single sound predicting the future

Sweet smiling village, loveliest of the lawn
now pale and hollow as a toothless yawn

Our mother played the piano and lovers
strolling by would pause peer into the cool room
where a young woman seemed lost in Debussy
and think that this was how life is meant to be
in a small town where you could walk anywhere
even away which is where our father walked:
Oh she'd have strangled him given half a chance!

Ill fares the land, to hastening ills a prey
where couples wake each day with less to say

I would bike to school up the steep hill around
the grand Hasken house where Mrs H had shot
the Chairman of the Board of Education
by accident (*Like hell* our father whispered
before he left thinking perhaps that Mother
would get ideas) the school composed of large stones
and small bones jelled in adolescent aspic

But now the sounds of population fail,
except around the mall or in the jail

Like a moth to its flame I often circle
by our empty house stop and get out my heart
that scarred philanderer jumping like a kid
again Today a fat spider sat spinning
her CD between our telephone wire
and laundry line and her song told me plainly
everything I loved was foolish and dying

The varnished clock that clicked behind the door
still ticks to me from time's diminished shore

Certainly we meant well like the citizens
of every town Pristina Columbine
Kabul Who doesn't want the good life with friends
at table the children safe music swelling
the air around us? Yet blades bloom in our hands
natural as daisies: the world addicted
to metal fitted for flesh like key to lock

But times are altered; trade's unfeeling train
shoots up our veins like moral novocain

We have a photo of our parents Father
on his back arms perpendicular Mother
doing a handstand on *his* hands the godly
strength and trust of that Olympian moment
all we can ask of life Anything more like
a happy ending perhaps seems…piggish Still
to see her dazed eyes today: unbearable

In all my griefs—and God has given my share—
the worst is this: that hope creates despair

Driving this morning I saw three men smoking
on top of a building-in-progress tiny
and soft against the iron beams The town is
dying streets yawn yet offices still sprout like
weeds with only people 'downsized' beauty gouged:
the pledged horn of plenty cheapened and betrayed
Triumphant parking lots cough through oily mouths

233

O Mother Father underneath the wave
we only wished for worlds beyond the grave

BILL MEISSNER

Ten Seconds Left in the High School Championship Game: James Dean Shoots the Basketball from Half Court

The game's always tied, just a few seconds left,
and his feet are always tiptoeing along the out-of-bounds lines.
To stop or to go, that's the question. To be
caught in this Indiana town all your life, acting
your way down Main Street, or not to be.
He's just seventeen, and the basketball in his palms weighs
as much as the whole earth. He can hear the
hissing as if it's slowly losing air. *Just don't think about it,*
his coach always said. He glances for an instant
at the red lines he's been told to follow
when all the time his eyes were thinking green,
green, and he accelerates his silver Porsche from the stoplight.
He's suddenly older, not just a kid, because holding
this basketball and staring at the hoop, so far away,
has aged him. The muscles in his arm flex,
like when he'll drink that fast glass of beer just east of Eden,
when he'll sit on that railroad flatcar in the cold night air
and hold his head tightly
to keep it from exploding.
He balances the ball beneath his line of vision,
and the moons on his fingernails glow.
The hoop floats away like a smoke ring
from the cigarette he'll smoke in *Rebel Without a Cause,*
but right now, in his head he hears the crowd
chanting the countdown: 9, 8, 7. And the light turns green.
Accelerate: There's always just a few seconds left.

6, 5, 4. The ball rockets from his hands, arcs upward into
orbit. It flies so slowly
that thirty years pass
as it travels the distance of the dark wooden floor
which becomes convex, like the surface of the earth from outer
    space.
The ball arcs over America, over
everything James will never live to see:
a president—fouled hard in the back of the head—slouching
    forward,
the scuff marks of Vietnam, a man jumping from the moon's
surface and into soft lunar air, cities erupting.
All James can do now is watch
as the ball reenters the atmosphere and approaches the hoop,
the sparks tailing behind it like prayers. 3,2,1.

When James wakes, he's older, pulling himself from a tangle of
    sheets.
He light a cigarette, lathers his face with clouds, shaves.
He stares in the mirror at the dark rings under his eyes
and remembers the game as it was: just ten boys,
five on each side in a little game, shooting an old leather
    basketball
on a gym floor warped and pockmarked like any other.
Someone had to win, someone had to lose: there are no ties.
Just don't think about it. Go.
Before he strolls to his Porsche for the last time,
he rolls up a wrinkled T-shirt.
With a quick jump shot,
he lofts it across the room.
It lands dead center in the wash basket with a
swish.

MARIO MILOSEVIC

Doll, Still Living

In retirement, Barbie
spent her days
chain smoking unfiltered Camels
and watching soap operas.

She understood the characters
and their problems.
Honey, she'd say to the tv,
dump the dickless bastard.
You can do better.

Once, years after her
last public appearance,
she was called before
a congressional committee
to speak on the issue
of plastic surgery
being covered by Medicare.

I owe my career
and all that I am
to polymer technology
she testified.

As she walked to
her limousine to leave
The Capitol some of her
local fans tried to push
past her bodyguards.

We love you, they shouted.

(no stanza break)

Retirement Barbie raised
her stiff arm and waved
her hand like a zombie.

Her fans bounced up
and down and screamed
like teenage girls at
a Beatles concert.

Barbie's limo driver
waited for her to
finish signing autographs
then he handed her a tissue
which she used to wipe away
her imaginary Barbie tears.

Thanks Ken, she sniffled,
you glorious, hopeless,
fucked-up wonder.

SUSANNA MISHLER

Women's Room

When it seemed empty you gagged and vomited
in another stall and I listened, with my shorts at my knees
to this sound of your body shrinking,

felt it tumble into my chest. It went on until I imagined
you might not be standing there anymore, reduced to a dot
above a toilet. Never small enough.

But you walked out in flesh so real I could have reached
over and smoothed your shirt collar. How red you were
when you saw me by the sinks;

I almost told you then about the woman who
puts Sweet 'N' Low in her hummingbird feeders,
just to speak of something more peculiar.

Because I couldn't do in that moment what I really wanted,
which was to draw from my pocket and press in your hand
a bright set of keys

to a Continental convertible, so you could walk out
on all this porcelain, peel through the knotted suburbs
and onto a desert highway—

blasting the radio, undoing the threads
that keep you so tightly sewn, and
                    taking up as much space as you can.

MICHAEL MOTT

Life Magazine

The worst things we learned from LIFE
in the cupboard, part of the built-in bookcase
to the right of the fireplace in the library.

Ethiopia, China, Spain
were supposed to be safe from our prying:
VooDoo dances in Haiti, thieves
having their hands cut off
in a public square of Yemen,
Crystal Palace Fire, Crystal Night,
the assassinations of Dollfuss, of Ernst vom Rath.

The front garden was given over
to orange marigolds, blue lupines,
the curtains in the library
were blue and orange, in a picture
over the mantlepiece a blue crow
picked over oranges with its beak.

The very details of our days
practised non-intervention.

Week by week copies entered
the cupboard, their covers
red for blood, white, grays
edged with swastika black.

In the end, we got away with nothing,
suffered shame three times over:
for the crimes, Guernica, the Rape of Nanking,
Dachau; for the awe and excitement we couldn't escape;
and for stealing, like those thieves in Yemen.

MICHAEL MOTT

Wasting Nothing

A sunspotted bridle path
idled between birches.
I was unsure when I took it,
afraid of the heat, the glare,
the smell of bracken
like something beaten to death.

I was afraid in my stomach.
I was afraid in my hands.
Behind my eyes
I was afraid.

I watched sparrows peck, peck,
turn horsedung after the riders passed;
peck, peck at stones, the underside of a slab.

They won't escape. I knew that.
Heat makes a prison for us all.
Putrid among dead leaves
were the severed heads of foxes.

Who has the strength to lift the grille,
look straight up into a cool, blue sky
and is it seagulls who fly there
or do fish float belly-upwards
pressed against glass?

At seven I asked too many questions
when my anger was all I had left,
an anger without a source.
I carried it everywhere
holding it in front of me
wasting nothing.

JOHN T. MUIR

Aplikation 4 the Post Off Gard Dog at Cellarscale Nuclear Reprocheesing Plant

Sire or Madman
I am just a very poore man
who in these tying times
-& despite some youthful petty krimes-
am honestlie honest

(and with Wyfe & familee
of 5 grilles and 2 buoyes)

am now sinking into despear
becos of hunger and deeprevation
(& wiv anuther chield on the wey!)

Thinke yorselfe…if U were ME…
(an but for the grace of Godde…)

U'd be prepaird 2 b
Anythink to feed those hear
(& the one about 2 apeare!)

I can growle & barke
I kan weight tense an snarle
an fighte on all 4s in the sunlite
or in the cole hole darke.

I don't want much pey
Just a few bobb sum scrappes
& a doggee bag perhaps
-to tek home at the end
off the odd day.

The houres ken b long or kould b short
-wotevere- trust me plees.
I'll not dessport meself out off line.
Just czech on me at eny time
& yorll find me thear
-or thereabouts.

Ive no religoos kneeds
I don't hav a Union —or eny Jews.

Isle take kash in hande if U prefear
-or…An openn chek each weekend will do,
Thursdey of fridey would be fine 2!

I'm braveharte & loyal & won't grumbel,
I get on well with other dogges
-& oh yes I don't tek Drugges
or mix wiv lowlyfe Thugges.

Weeknisses? Oh yiss.
I yusd 2 drink…
b4 my Wyfe
-but once the kiddies came
I reaLynned my Lyfe.

Pleese Mr Deesishion Makker,
Giv us all a break.
True I'm very poore
An not that brighte
but I'd lik
a reel chance to dance
in a peying lyfe.

Imagine the smile on my Wyfe
at me being emploid at last
after all the dissapointmints of the past
a door that doesn't slamme shut an fast!

ROBERT NAZARENE

Church

> *"I ride alone. It's a great feeling of freedom,*
> *noise, wind and speed."*
> --Thomas "Road Kill" Anderson

The glint

of a chrome sunrise: begun
as mustard seed.

Being there: if only
because someone said: *No.*   Alone.

Eschew cages. Make no explanations.
(There are none). No false moves.

Keep your eyes on the road.
Don't be fake.

Be invisible. Explore.
Handle business. Never get off.

Commend yourself to God—
to your *ministry*.

ROBERT NAZARENE

The Anointing

*"A liar is always
lavish of oaths."*
   ---Pierre Corneille

*Assalam Alakum, Alakum
Assalam*---May the wondrous
Peace of Islam

be with you
& yours---all about you
& in you & through you

amongst the lilies
& briers of Shechum;
as you dip your oars

into the mirror
of Galilee & roam
the olive groves

which girdle Samaria
& Besan. May you
find the glorious

Peace of Allah---aglow,
in the lapis
sky above Hebron;

beside the poplars, shimmering
by the lakeshore
of Dothan;

flowing,
as a river,
between the pages

of our holy Koran;
beneath the hallowed
stones of Bethany

& Penuel; a prayer,
invisible, beneath your seat,
on the ride to morning

kaddish---
aboard your south-
bound bus

from Jerusalem
to Adullam.

ROBERT NAZARENE

H E A V E N ' S S C E N T

Churchmouths & weenie-drinkers love me.
Injuns, too. The Baptist, John, says
I do him proud.

> *"I'd like to buy the world*
> *a Coke--& keep it company.*
>
> *I'd like to..."*

One block north on Powell Street—
above The Westin St. Francis Hotel,

a sign reads:

> JESUS GAVE MONEY TO THE POOR.
> A MAN NAMED FRANCIS, WALKED
> THE STREETS OF ASSISI, A BEGGAR.

(The bellhop is bringing
your bags right up.)

RENÉE ELLEN OLANDER

Rhinos Got No Luck

Yesterday, a ten-year old newcomer to a zoo
fought her new mate & broke
out of her cage, galumphed
off zoo grounds, chased by three
trucks of vets armed
with tranquilizer guns & one rifle—
& what sort of luck was it
that only the kill shot
between the eyes could calm her?

And there were a pair of rhinos shipped
from Cleveland to China as a gift
who died on the seventh day of their flatbed
truck drive in one hundred degrees
of dehydration. Until the zoo
can find replacement rhinos,
they'll show the stuffed carcasses,
which is cheaper than watering rhinos,
and there's profit from the magic
horns, whose likeness in wax
convince from a distance.

And at my local zoo, one of two rhinos
swallowed a racquetball
which blocked its intestines,
and it died like dozens do a year
--or was that the hippos?—
from balls tossed playfully
into their confines (so maybe
you've even killed one yourself).

I know it sounds crazy, but why
can't I get the dry-mouthed rhinos
on a flatbed in China off my mind?
How they remind me of a little boy
lost on his bike in the business district
who asked me once for water
and what was his way home?

BARBARA PAPARAZZO

Falling Through the Cracks on a Snowy Evening in Western Massachusetts

Watching an old Sakyajit Ray film
I become entranced by a young woman named
Durga from the ancient city of Varanasi
who lies in bed with a fever, dying, when
all at once she opens her arms to her mother,
like a blossom to the sun,
a gesture so simple,
so honest,
it must be the letter A
in the alphabet of gestures,
like a river rushing to the ocean,
like the great Ganga itself,
it is as perfect as green pears spread
on a white cloth in an open window—
then I remember,
daughterless,
I am holding onto a
broken rope.

R. A. PAVOLDI

Fibonacci's Number

9/11/01

It's like the dream where all your teeth loosen
and roll around in your mouth, and if you don't
awaken they fall from your mouth like stones
or bricks, or keyboard keys, strange confetti.

I was talking to the young woman from
the house in back I haven't seen in years,
I was in the garden, she was out early
in pajamas not expecting to see

anyone, she filled me in on her family,
about starting her new job in New York,
occasionally tugging at her tee-shirt,
standing barefoot in the fallen apples

radiant with her dark hair pulled back,
I apologized for the kids' fort spilling
into her grandmother's yard, she smiled
and said it reminded her of when she was small,

and later that day she left for New York
right before the big rain. That was
a month ago, and today driving home
from work I saw another young woman

sitting on a blanket on a front lawn
with a little girl, maybe it was
her little sister, or niece, or maybe
her daughter if she had had her very young,

it was like they were waiting for the leaves
to fall, I thought, how many vacation
snapshots and family pictures, how many
messages on Post-It Notes, how many

inspirational blurbs, and Dilbert cartoons
tacked on partitions, how many copiers
and water coolers, telephones still warm
with conversations, and fifty-thousand

computers each with 64 megs of RAM
is at least a trillion bites of memory,
and if every person had a contact list
like they ask you to make when you get hired

to sell life insurance, every relative
and doctor, your mechanic and barber,
your accountant, priest or rabbi, you should
have a list of at least five-hundred people,

and if every one of those thousands had
a list of five-hundred people, that would be
at least a vigintillion bits of memory
a googolplex of pieces of dreams,

suspended at 9/11, the red
speedometer needle of a Corvette
that hit a tree in 1967,
stuck at 120, one tooth still in the dash

when they towed it to the lot by the
garage the next day, everyone gathered
to look and talk about the things that kid
would never see, never do, just one life,

imagine this sequence of thousands
loosened and rolling around in your mouth,
then falling like strange confetti,
like infinity, as ash.

REBECCA HAZELTON PENNELL

Temporary

It is the moment before the burning house gently implodes
into glitter and sawdust, a slow afterglow against the blackening
    sky.
The actors are in place; the child screams as she should;

the dog howls from the flame ringed window frame, paws singed,
and only the father is not in his place—
drunk and asleep in the favorite armchair,

or perhaps heroically lost in the flames, while he tosses
the charring baby from blistering hand to hand.
One potato, two potato, three—

and no one on the wet lawn hears anything
because no one is on the lawn to hear.
The neighbors mind their own business.

This was your favorite part of the movie. The swelling
of the soundtrack made you laugh—no tragedy
manufactured could compare to the mundane

causes—misplaced keys and the stove let on,
an iron forgotten, or even the freakish
ball lighting incident, the babysitter burning

on the couch, the television remote still in her hand.
Or you, in an unexpected cameo. You whistle
as you walk away. The sloshing gas can keeps time.

SIMON PERCHIK

*

It takes an aim—one chair, another
then higher—you make a tree
trembling in the snow, bare
from the light that peels off
surprised by the sudden thirst and ceiling

--you win a *Beck* and the bartender
keeps wiping away some stream
and you circle the thin glass
filled with unbearable height

--you turn back
and how much like winter it sounds
and something you never expected would hold.
These chairs will too
and somewhere on the pile the dead
are stretching their necks
--you reach inside the glass
try to dry the singing past midnight
the stream that clogs your breath and fingers.

ELLEN PERLESS

You are Wearing

your fur coat
and your long legs

walking your model's loopy walk.

You foxy little face
is not too smart
but it is lovely;

your almond eyes
are someplace very else.

And you
are wearing
your fur coat.

And you are off, off to the ball.
The ball is all.

And even if last night
you stuck your tongue into my mouth,
well, what of that?

Right now, the ball is all.
Your long legs, your loping loopy walk.
Off to the ball.

Today, you look at me like I was god.
In a few years,
you're history.

Luna, my moony love, my watery star,
my torch, my self, my flame,
            you'll break my heart,
            you little bitch.
You're all the same.

TERESA PFEIFER

The Guest

Encouragement had disappeared in Krakow.
And so it was.

We watched movies to suspend the portentousness of the New
    Year.
When you flew away, I recalled a happy smell: baby spittle can be
    soothingly sweet.

To pass the time, you wrote to say that a big change
in perspective had occurred in your town.

People began looking down.
I crawled into your bed and burrowed.

You are a distant part of me, that I know.
Does the cello understand its bow?

I found one half dozen uses for *treacly*.
When I rose from my sorrow,

I ached for the moonlight and thought of someone's shoe
forgotten among the kelp at the edge of the sea.

TERESA PFEIFER

Across the Darkness

In the hallway, the roses scroll dark
flower after dark flower.
There is no once again.
The moan in the apple orchard.
The room without furniture.
The minnows' home.
In an empty theater
the floor needs scrubbing
and flooding. Unconscious laboring to surface.
Eisenstein's cascade of coats, boots,
and a baby. The wheel teetering on the stairs.
Waves of would be white petals like soggy umbrellas.
Blossoms of light lap the surface.
The odor of ash. The flicker of film.
No one tries to hide in the hat that floats.
Night sky and night forest.
Blonde girl deep inside the factories.
Afraid to leave, to be dinner
for the roaming dogs.
A lady and a gentleman in a carriage
on their way home.
The horse clip clops on the stone road.
The vines wind their way around her ankles.
How can she sleep making movies of wallpaper?

JOHN PURSLEY III

The Reigning Sound

When the first shots echo through the intersection
Between the Diamond Theatre & the First Baptist
Youth Center like bottle-rocket reports
Or Buddy Rich rim-shots attacking the band
Like a drill sergeant—*you motherfuckers*
Are suckin' all over this joint!—
The bars have already begun to filter out
Into the street, & new assemblages are forming
And huddle to cars, discussing rides & after-hours,
And my own car was idling beautifully in the light
Holding red.
        Then, running. Then screaming.
Water oozing up into the ear, & everything is floating.
Each note blurring—next, next—in a phrase
Not of this world, & people pour past my windows
Like spooked horses, broken—their mouths gnashing
At the names of loved ones, as the dark shapes
Of their bodies disappear like sheets
Of sound, like walls to blood, to brick, to mortar,
Behind the eyes, the socket's hollow.
                And now
Two of them are fighting, swinging their bodies
Like heavy fists.
        Though they could have been lovers,
Could have been dancing under the stars reeling
In the upper echelons, the halogens humming
And the band settling into itself behind the big beat
Of the drums, Buddy's quick snaps of snare,
Impossible, driving. Night, all around them
Sliding through the dirty streets, through gutters,
The knuckled throats of steam,

(no stanza break)

Sliding over rooftops, along the canal & river basin,
The false-front stores & mini-malls, coiling
The spires of the Trinitarian church,
Closing in on the distance holding them there
Clinging to each other's bodies.
                              And one by one
Both will fall—the first into the other's arms,
Lifeless as Michelangelo's exhausted skin
In the Sistine Chapel, held fast by Saint Bartholomew,
Disillusioned, limp.
                    The second to follow—
The shots resounding still, as if from the earth itself,
Coming in triplets, sixteenths.

YOSEFA RAZ

Blue and White is My Color

My hands are dusted with pepper,
I can't bring them near my face.
Coordinates for soldiers take over the nature trails.
History textbooks have buried villages alive.

I also played in the scrubby lots between apartment buildings
sticky with anise and milkweed;
gathered leaves to paste in my season-book,
crayoned underneath: "the colors of autumn";

drew pictures of the wall around our city
on Reunification of Jerusalem Day,
and sang, "All the country is flags, flags, flags."
"Blue and white is my color," and it was not the color of clouds.

I also owned one cotton uniform, two Dacron uniforms,
and the dog tags said my name.
I didn't learn war off a man's body
but neither did a man's rippling skin teach me peace.

I studied Arabic like the rest of you, instead of French
and like the rest of you I remember nothing.
The Minister of Technology and Agriculture toured the country
We can say in Arabic as a party trick, or to admit the presence of
    ghosts.

Like the rest of you, I jump at sirens.
I ridicule American tourists who get cheated by taxi-drivers.
I save tea bags. I recognize all the sad songs on army radio.
I hide my wrong passport, my mother's thick American accent.

Don't tell me to renounce you, when I've lived
with the women of Rechavia, been spied on through keyholes.

Don't tell me to renounce my right to meddle,
holler as loud as the studio audience at the what-will-be talk
    shows.

Let's gather weeds for our Sabbath meal.
The weeds in this city are like the goose and lamb of another
    city—
enough to feed all our refugees,
whose ill-fitting gold teeth make it difficult to chew.

How many dead today? "Oh the situation,"
we groan and settle into our Bauhaus chairs.
Channel one, channel two.
The trees are turning blue and white with sorrow.

CHRISTINE RHEIN

Artist Maurice Bennett Explains His "Burning Desire"

*-a picture of the Mona Lisa on the side
of a building using 2,124 slices of toast*

I know what you're thinking—
wasn't it bad enough?—her likeness
stamped on socks and shower curtains,
shaped into cookie jars, mustached
in milk or with matching goatee,
morphed into *Mona Lewinsky*
and pink Muppet *Mona Pigga*.
But this is different. This is Art, inspired,
yes, by an overtoasted piece of *Wonder*,
my knife scraping away charred crumbs,
revealing flesh tones underneath—
bread gone *chiaroscuro*, features
emerging from shadow, patterns of singe.
Though don't think it's easy, browning
thousands of squares to specific hues,
or burning them—black and blacker—
without setting off the smoke alarm,
and arranging all those right angles,
so unlike the contours of her shoulders,
her bosom, which alone measures 18 by 27
luscious slices—my happiest days
on the scaffold, engulfed, dwarfed
by her dough-beige cleavage.
Picture the tension, the crowd watching
as I assembled her giant eyes watching them
no matter where they stood. And then the vast
mystery of her smile, lips I longed to kiss
despite their yeast-formed craters.

(*no stanza break*)

263

It's true—I love her. I've even tasted
her, her crunch melting on my tongue,
her voice whispering in my dreams
where, there too, I protect her from mold
and birds, as I magically float about her,
my Lisa, my darling, my toast.

SUZANNE RHODENBAUGH

The Last Stuff

Mamma's dark red satin evening bag, fringed at the bottom.
Her pale blue silk bedjacket, cutwork above the breasts.
Her hand mirror—mother of pearl on the back,
amber round the front frame. Her lipsticks—Beautiful Pink.

Her unreadable Bible, one inch square.
Her driver's license from 1951,
her crud-encrusted tea set with busted bases,
the doctor's slides of her eyeballs: all this stuff

a sister half-threw, half-packed in a box to me
with my uncashed check for postage,
my Girl Scout handbook, the crumbling head
of my favorite doll, and a few dead roaches.

See, after Mamma died, nothing would suffice
--no funeral, no memorial service—
'cause nothing was tried. I heard those who decided
put her ashes in a pewter urn and buried them in Georgia,

but I can't swear to its truth. I still say
--though I hightailed it gone
some thirty-five years ago, and was the absolute
baby to boot—all Mamma's children

should have gotten together
to eat acorns, drink vinegar,
pick at scabs, sit on the hot asphalt
of the tacky town we come from, and burn.

SUZANNE RICHARDSON

These Things

After the day is done.
We are still reliving a corner of poverty.
The thin women in thrift store dresses.
The pinched face of a man
    staring into hard times.
Everywhere the embarrassment
    of turning to charity.
Small children sick with hunger.
Mothers frantic.
Grocery bags filled with donated food
    lined up in rows in the hallway.
The last check signed
    and the last shelter called.

We are left with these things:
The pain of lifting, of holding, of sitting,
    typing, cradling a phone to an ear
      or a crying child to a shoulder.
The crusts of sandwiches.
The residue of many feet on the carpet
    and of many fingers on the door handle.
The skin of dried coffee in the coffee pot.
A new day before us.

JAY ROGOFF

In Camera

Eternal life via a hinged wood box,
      a silvered plate, a man drunk
     on the stink
         of visionary chemicals:
               pneumonia, scarlet fever, a rheumatic
heart, anything plucks
           off a child of nine, leaving a thick
              Victorian glaze
          on its eyes,
       a bruise where its skull's
               been passionately kissed,
             a body perfectly composed
         for worship on the settee, no nervous tic
  or blink
        to blur the work
            of the daguerreotypist
aiming forever to fix
                nature
                here in the parlor.

Light's remains absorb us. Whatever reflects
     can illuminate
        the silver buried
deep in a dark box,
     sun banging on metal, a sleight
       to gong the spirit
back to our world, where artifacts
        (this corpse's dazzling image, ferried
          to new life in the palm)
            can, after full immersion
            in poison,

       (no stanza break)

                    thrive in a wood frame,
            a cold child offered
        on a cold, reflective plate.

From your frame
        on the piano
                you smile, Father,
        as if you didn't know
                        a grimmer image knocks
                        in my mind's dark box—
        a grayer picture,
        your face grisaille as old snow
into which your headlong frame,
                        like a filthy joke,
            a pratfall at a formal dinner,
                        lurched prone
                        and made a last impression.
            Neither gin nor
                        formaldehyde, not even
                    the polished, hand-joined oak
        coffin's casement window
            from which you cast your
                        frozen last look,
                    could put the trick
                        across, the bright illusion
you were at rest, or warm.

MICHAEL SALCMAN

Fish Talks, Town Buzzes—
New York Times, 3-15-03

For the sake of drama, it would be nice to think
Luis Novelo almost chopped his hand off
when the fish began to speak,
instead he dropped a rubber mallet used to stun
the carp with and fell against the wall
sliding on to slimy packing crates that covered
the floor. No one in Ecuador spoke Hebrew
but he knew it when he heard it
having worked in Mr. Rosen's shop
for seven years. He thought it was the devil
speaking in the cat's throat, thrown
from another room or from the slop sink,
from anywhere but a fish. He flung it back
into the ice box and still it spoke; Luis yelled
and soon enough Mr. Rosen heard it too—
the voice of God, he thought
or even Mr. Lifshitz, a holy man
who died last year, come back to fret about
his town and its morals.
Zalmen heard the old Hasid say "study Torah
and pray, the end is near". All those years
the man bought carp for Shabbos
and never said a word; now this!
How he hated those silvered lips!
Mr. Rosen tried to kill it with a cleaver
but the soul of Mr. Lifshitz bucked off
the counter and fell into the carp box,
snuggling down with its iced-off
brethren. Zalmen almost cut his thumb off
and had to be taken away in an ambulance.

(no stanza break)

A psychiatrist asked—
was it a Purim prank or a mass hallucination?
What does it mean when God's word
is made manifest in a twenty pound carp,
then butchered and sold for appetizer?
Months later, Luis was largely left alone
and Zalmen no longer answered his phone.
"Two men do not dream the same dream",
said Abraham Spitz, a lawyer. Or—
one man's god is another man's devil.

MICHAEL SALCMAN

Double Orange Car Crash

It's a lot like deciphering the symbols
in a Breughel; who are these smiling faces?
In a hundred years, I bet no one will hang
Andy's vanity portraits of starlets,
captains of commerce,
or society matrons in a museum,
each painted at forty thousand dollars a pop,
because no one will know their names,
just his.
They might not even hang our immortal
ephemera, those coke bottles, dollar signs
and faux boxes of Del Monte peaches
because he wasn't the first to press ink
through a screen or worship the transitory.
So not too much will last of his hipness
except a cool stare and his silver fright wig
in that cheap polaroid, silent and coy
about what he meant.
I know he loved their pure desperation,
that's what unites them, Liz and Jackie,
Elvis and Marilyn, with the bodies thrown
in a tree, the man jumping out of a building,
the head crushed by an orange and black
car wreck,
the skulls, guns and switchblades,
the red electric chairs and the self-portraits
with surgical scars.
Oh they'll remember Andy, all right
like Breughel and Bosch, our own Mr. Death.

DAVID SALNER

A Short Poem on the Shooting By Police of Charquisa Johnson, April 27, 2003, in Washington, DC

The police said she held a gun in the air
and refused to drop it. Her friend
said her hands were empty
except for the kiss she was blowing
her two children. They blew her lights out
but missed what was dangerous—
there it is, still blowing
high above the lights
of her city.

CINDY SAVETT

Rachel, my daughter
July 19, 1991 – May 26, 2000

Rachel: Patterns c 5

I am the blood of a child

the weight of a thread
under the mist

my face is hidden among thorns
    gray drippings from god

        salt tiles
        rage white on my tongue

exhumed by the wind
all the bones of eternity align fevers and sores
with the wooden gate

in the blue breath
I sleep.

Rachel: Patterns a 2

In the wild dance she is queen

the memory and the mist
a white dream upon her lips

scrim of leaves above her head
vines and the sky terrain

she sorts the rainfall and rotting words
through a veil of ten thousand screams

filters the prayer.

Rachel: Tiles a 3

Daybreak haunts
across from where the shining lies

casting
on watersand
canvases of block and paint.

Swearing away the memory of early dusk

resonant blue
element of the dark

I beat the steel frame.

LON SCHNEIDER

The Anatomy of Evil in Lawrence, Kansas

The elevator is out
at the Holiday Inn.

The concierge tries to convince you
there's a surcharge
to activate the phone

the water

the lights.

She waves your cash
announces your room number
and hands you a skeleton key.

All night long
children drown
in the heated pool.

You leave your shaving brush.

It will prove
nearly impossible to replace.

PETER SERCHUK

Yankee Stadium, 1965

Yom Kippur is how you separate
the Jews from the jews.
Not Chanukah or Purim with their latkes
and laughter, not Shavuo or Tu B'Shevat...
God himself can't remember the month.
And Rosh Hashana, holy as it is,
trumpets one more circle, a clean step forward,
as unJewish an idea as happiness itself.

But Yom Kippur, when we feast
on the same dust left to Moses above Canaan,
on the same dust that bore witness to
Hank Greenberg's giant shoes, that's when
we tell Him that we, the chosen ones, are here
to earn his blessings, to beg his forgiveness
no matter whose game or rules.
That's why today, World Series be damned,
that's handsome Don Drysdale on the mound
and not the hungry Jew, Sandy Koufax.

JACQUELYN SHAH

Here's to Refraction, Uncle Fred

It's not as though I didn't notice your heart, after all
you made it clear when you unshirted your chest, made me press
my nose against the glass, all beveled and windexed
I thought *oh,*
if only I could touch that meat-fist I could almost smell
(making me feel again
the joy of backyard grilling)   A sucker
for anything red and spasmic, I'm easily fed
I thought *ah,* looks like a moose ball, wanted to roll it
into my sweaty palm   You advertised it
as a two-for-one, deluxe and guaranteed   I lay
my cheek, as you insisted, against cool casing
pretending that cloistered rouge-pot wanted to give of itself
imagining how rosy-glowed I'd be then, like a dawn
on the dance floor of you   how we might two-or-three-step
into midnight's favorite fog in tux
and boutonniere, slinky sequined dress and orchid
I had an image of it riding on the backseat, leather, of a Lexus
-RX300, 3-litre V6, 24-valve engine, intelligent variable valve
timing, automatic with sequential shift   Suddenly
I thought, I'll write a little poem to praise it
as though it were a fat angel in a scarlet gown
a chain purse full of peppermints, hot placenta stew
You raised my head, held my hair with one hand, pointed
with the other   I saw one red cent, a port-wine stain, a lobster
    claw
looked again, a bulgy circus nose, veiny scabrous nose, a wattle
chigger chili dog bloody gauze a blotch a nipple jello jerky
    Spam—*Uncle!*
I jerked…you let me go…my heart was pounding…I thought
    ugh…
I passed out, dreamed of gladiolas, poplars, thunder, courage…

KATHLEEN SHEEDER

The St. Regis

Heaven, I believe this, heaven
will be a luxury hotel,
like the St. Regis on 55th at Fifth Avenue
with Caswell-Massey soaps in the bath
and turn-down service
and a foil-wrapped chocolate
laid on my pillow
by the invisible hand of God.

And there, in the morning
I will drink mimosas
one, and then carelessly another
and go to the Metropolitan in the afternoon
and maybe I will wear gloves
and maybe I will take my pug dog,
and maybe the pug will wear something too.
We will visit the Greek galleries and the Roman,
and the Temple of Dunder
and the European Wing
and I will smile, but kindly
not derisively, not here,
at the sweet besotted wrong-headed effort
of all these men over all these ages
the afterlife full of curly clouds,
and firmament and yellow light,
lovely, yes, but where
is the forgiving carpet, the thirsty robe,
the capacious chair,
the fat book with all its possibility
and room service knocking softly on the door?
Michelangelo, it is true,

(no stanza break)

knew more than most
and before I go, in the gift shop
I will buy a postcard of God
touching the finger
of the concierge of the St. Regis
Where later, in the hallway
impulsively, I will turn to the guest next door
who, as fate would have it,
hurt me horribly once.
And I will reach out my large long flowery
magnanimous arms
with my boxy pocketbook swinging on my wrist
and I will forgive him, finally
and he'll turn to someone
from the room next to his
and she'll turn to someone
and then heaven will resound
with the music of doors flinging open
and loud forgetting and holy laughing.

DEREK SHEFFIELD

Bigness Is It's Own Reward

--from an advertisement for Robert Wadlow's
grave in Alton, Illinois

The tallest man in the world
was a talker, his five-foot
mother soon under-
stood as she watched him grow
conversational. Can you believe
a TV tower sauntering up
and up through sparks
of snapped electrical lines
to intone *How's it goin'?*
like a downpour of oil drums?
He longed for a lover
and settled for accounting
until his fingers no longer fit
the keys. And when the shoes
he modeled across Long Island
began to pinch, he found
finally he was perfect
at nothing. If he stopped
and stood still as an American elm
between the fattest woman,
who blushed wide as a sunset,
and the shortest man, Tom,
in a goatee, he was something,
someone's discovery, a clock tower
ticking hugely backstage,
muttering nervous repetitions
of *Red leather, Yellow leather.*
As the monster, he made people
feel cracks in the cliffs
of far places, and every boy and girl

(no stanza break)

jerked from those dead moon eyes.
And every night for twenty-two years,
stretched across long beds, he drifted off
to the clangs and cusses
of his soot-faced bones
working the swing shift.

FLOYD SKLOOT

Yeshiva in the Pale, January, 1892

Early morning, as Cossacks on horseback
circled the old wooden synagogue, chants
seeped out like smoke through the walls. Black
hatted elders inside shut their eyes and danced
in circles of their own before the holy ark.
Prayer deepened the air as one fat soldier nailed
the Tsar's seal to the door: CLOSED. Then a spark
cast from somewhere near the rising sun sailed
across the wintry sky, encircling soldier
and temple, nuzzling rooftree, gable, beam.
It found the place where mingled rage and dream
were draft enough to let a wildfire smolder.
One moment shadows questioned the winter dark
and next moment the answer arrived in flame.

TOM SMITH

Michael Jackson to Become a Priest
(*Weekly World News*, March 18, 2003)

Under the surgeon's knife the world lies dreaming
of wakeful beauty in high Catholic drag. It isn't
Diana Ross. It isn't Elizabeth Taylor. It's Michael
Jackson wafted upon an altar of chorus boys, flanked
by a chorus of altar boys, angels, putti, each white
superpellicium glowing afloat over neon dreamland.

And Michael's own·white surplice unfurls like ermine
cumulo-nimbi unrolling round his fancied limbs and torso
and the tumble of black skirts, his cassock that gathers
like fog from which prim feet peer forth
over the rim of the dreaming world.

Michael's raised hands frame his smile
as he anticipates (as we anticipate)
an elaboration of vestments and accessories: amise,
alb and cincture, chasuble, dalmatic, humeral
veil, stole, pluvial, morse. Pyx or ciborium to contain,
monstrance to display the host. Gold and gem-encrusted
thurible exuding myrrh or frankincense.

I was never an altar boy but I did often kneel
before the peacock priest and his pigeon acolytes,
my bird brain dreaming to receive the host, my knees
naked and scabby, some buttons broken from my fly,
my short pants faded, and God on the tip of my tongue
like a word nearly remembered.

In the world's dumb dream of Father Michael,
the altar boys are faceless for no reason.

(no stanza break)

And in my recollection of any summer
Sunday morning I perceive at last we are all
faceless as a wafer, as white bread.
And neither wine nor water turns.

KATHERINE SONIAT

On the Steppe

Dying, his spirit moved to another level,
looking for a place to rest the thoughts.
All night I blessed him on the journey
then emptied a cellophane of stars,
silver and gold dropping down
through my glass of tea.
Hermits in a pale universe,
each fleck sinking to a dimension
where it is good to be less.

I watched his eyes begin to wander the dark
like a town. We joined forces, no hint of light
on the streets, nothing to amuse or sadden.
The sole movie played in another language.
Lear in embattled black and white. In Russian
he raved on the moonlit steppe, motioned
to the wind not to turn its back.

GARY SOTO

One Day in May

With one window of the labor bus gone,
Wind stirred the lunches
Of men with puckered brows.
I look in my lunch bag—
Five crackers speckled
With salt. I licked my lips
And lapped one of the saltines.
Brother asked, "What are you doing?"
He was holding onto the seat in front
Of him. "Brunch," I said,
Then laughed, brunch the one
Word I had learned in English
The previous week. I licked
One side, then the other,
And returned the cracker to my bag,
Soggy from the strapping of my tongue.
Outside, the beet and cotton fields,
And darkness where the sloe-eyed
Headlights didn't cut a path.
When the labor bus bumped over a pothole,
We all screamed. The wind picked up,
Flapping the sleeves of our flannel shirts.
"Rough winds do shake the darling buds
of May," I quoted to the lunch
In my lap. My brother asked,
"What did you say?" Shakespeare,
I answered, this too learned in English,
A line to confuse a girl
In the third row. Brunch
And Shakespeare, and me
Saying "Cheerio, Jeeves" to the bus driver,

(no stanza break)

287

With wind still flapping
In his hair. I stepped
Off the bus, lunch under
My arm, and picked up my hoe.
Beets that day, plants with their arms up
And all slaughtered by the time the saltine crackers
Were eaten, by the time
The lucky rich were sitting down
To the lovely morsels of High Tea.

GARY SOTO

Treatment for Law Enforcement Mini-Series

The police found an arm and foot in a zipped-up gym bag,
Then a torso and three fingers in another.
A black bird perched on the head two miles away,
Head on a pile of hard pan no rain could rinse into gold.
The severed parts appeared in a canal. The piece work began
Where the frogs had gone quiet, their spiteful tongues gathering
    goo.
This was a Thursday night murder   .
Under a fishbowl sky. The rookie cop saluted his captain.
He bagged these bloodless body parts
And lay them on a metal table with one of its wheels gone.
His job done, the rookie circled the block in his cruiser
For that crime and others. He did what he was told,
A half-eaten burger in his lap, French fries the length of fingers.
Then he saw: pedestrians had hatchets in their stares,
Anger in the black and white punks, the Korean liquor store
    owners,
The Pakistani cab drivers, the Mexican gardeners on their knees,
And the middle-aged yoga teacher, her contorted legs behind her
    head,
Nearly severed from her body by the look of things.
The rookie swallowed his cold burger.
He sped up his cruiser: in the rearview mirror,
He followed the arc of knives and hatchets hurled at him—
Tomahawks of hatred from the mailman
And poorly dressed social worker,
The giddy-up college students on scooters.
His breathing rushed. A homeless woman buried a fork
In his forehead. With each blink,
The spot of blood behind his eyes flashed.

(no stanza break)

289

At a red light, he brushed French fries from his lap,
Fingers, he thought, burnt fingers
Falling and the bodies long gone.

MARCELLA SPRUCE

What Roy Orbison Can Say

Lonely is a subject only for Roy Orbison,
a sad man who knew something about "just one,
thanks." Lonely is the echo chamber living

room. Lonely is the inexorable silence that looms
over dinner for one. The lid of that dish
a matriarchal grandmother always wished

would serve another generation just clinks
like a prison door. "Lonely," we never think
to write to the alumni news. We don't believe

the girl who dressed in black to dance 'til three
will be no lover, no matriarch, and a companion only
of telephone and television and computer screen.

MARCELLA SPRUCE

Why The Times *Prints the Weather in Afghanistan*

Gamely, *The Times* now prints the weather in Afghanistan.
We, who have learned to find Kabul and Kandahar, and been

startled by the memory of that long-forgotten scandal,
the Khyber Pass, can now know that it is seasonable there,

warm in the south, cold in the mountains, as the bombs,
like migrating Canada geese, seize temperate moments to fly.

In this ordinary season in ordinary time, the leaves are still falling
on the knots of mourners who gather in Middletown and
    Greenwich

and Marblehead. The widows and widowers and orphans must
ponder the strange and ancient terminology of their new
    condition.

They are not starving, these orphans. This young widow does
    not pull
a burqa around her to ward away the cold. But the winds

that blow sandstorms into the delicate machinery of journalism
also shake the loosened leaves of stolid northern maples.

In the Barents Sea, the dolphins say goodbye to their sad guests
on the Kursk. In the mountains, the mujahedeen create new

widows. The dust still floats above Manhattan, they say, and,
    even as the geese
fly south, we study intently the salmon-pink and Nile-green map

that shows the weather in Afghanistan.

KAREN STANISLAW

tAlENT
MIGht wAIt
iN YouR hOlStER,
anD tRUE to yOUr oWN mEMory
YOU HAVE to aDmit
yOU'vE beEN liMpiNG WitH it.
pARts dOn'T flOat,
THEY SuiCiDE as AppENDAge
pLAgUeing bAllEt
tHAT KEPt yOU
GeNtlE.

KAREN STANISLAW

Brooch

```
CAN you lovE A *tRiNKEt likE
A BrothER, And wRAp youR
ARMS ArouND it, AND COVEt it iN
yOUR thoughts, AND plAN for its pLACE
     iN yOUR HotEL?!  Yes!, yEs you
cAN.  --  dEpENDiNg ON youR
ZEAL, And the iMBALANCED NATURE
          OF youR SociAl liFE.
```

S. ASHER SUND

Unwritten

They're playing Christmas music in the kosher bagel shop.
The phone rings on television and I pick it up.
A man gets hit by an ambulance
and dies. The interstate from not far away
can sound like a waterfall. There's a fire
in the fire station. Why always skinny people
on ads for fast food restaurants? Skinny people
with great complexions. I'm getting rained on
in my shelter. My sleeve only covers
one third of my cup. The boss
preaches on the theology of the company.
The pastor talks about the business of God.
The psychiatrist is crazy. The fish is out of water.
The doctor calls in sick. The hairdresser
is bald. The bird decides to walk. Two
is now one. I lost my contact. I sent you away. Why
because. I'm completely fractured. I'm working
out of order. I was born to die. The silence is deafening.
Even the blind can see this bus is fully empty. And I get off.

EMILY SUNDERLAND

Strawberries

I ate them
fifty two pieces
red and white and cold
while you sat on the floor
in the other room counting change,
'clink clink, clink clink' and they reminded me of love,
sweet in each bite and I almost felt satisfied
almost alright with the
jingling fact that you
had just about
forgotten
me.

EMILY SUNDERLAND

The Ascension

We would be going fast, laughing, dizzied by the hum
of the highway. I will take the blame. Maybe I was reminding
you of the book you left behind, or taking an eyelash
from your cheek, when the other car appeared. We could be
holding hands when things get quiet. I would be next to you,
as our heads push forward, slowly, into the dashboard,
twisting like balls of wet sugar, then back up again,
gravity carrying us, motheringly. Our knees would slide up
and shut like fists, then release, like a bud opening and closing.
It will be peaceful, head on, a false moment, the space
in between two thoughts. Do not worry my dear, my sweet heart,
my left half. I will be thinking of you more, of your chin bruising
against the wheel, of your body lodged for flight, tense and brave,
a buffalo at the edge of his cliff. We will know nothing of the
momentum of the car spinning its body like a top, like a flower
twirled between two fingers, until the guardrail, until seconds
bring us over it, getting rid of us, keeping us together.

KIRK SWEARINGEN

The Boy in Me

The boy in me is out to destroy me,
thinking he can still have his way with all,
and he's having an easy time of it,

since aging is really not becoming
but is all about *becoming*, which is
difficult and often terrifying.

The boy sits in a chair in a hallway,
and he reads or hums a tune, swings his legs.
Truth is, I don't know how he spends his time.

He's just hanging around, waiting his turn.
When I'm fearful, he jumps up with a whoop
and starts making all sorts of plans for me,

ways for me to annihilate this old form,
which seems to bring him endless displeasure.
Of course, I've not lived up to his grand hopes.

That's his litany, his sing-song chiding.
He doesn't realize how busy I am,
how I have children of my own to raise.

And such a taskmaster, for just a kid!
To drown out this voice, men go to great lengths;
some succeed entirely, and are old;

others keep the boy around for his spark,
though he is often unmanageable
and is well known for speaking out of turn.

He wants me dead, if I won't let him live.
And so I allow him to divert me
from a day at work to a museum

or from mundane chores out to the deep wood.
The trick, I find, is getting him to work,
to do the chores he is happy to do,

like this poem he's writing, as I speak.

TONI THOMAS

Pink Flamingos

Every winter when the wind rose
my mother scooped snow away
dug bulbs into the hard earth
rammed the long metal legs of
the pink flamingos into the place
Christmas lights might be.

Come June
tulips lifting in a faint breeze
her web chair appeared
never left the side of the front stoop
not till the rust of autumn rains
claimed it
and she abandoned her heart.

Who remembers the tulips
the shy throated irises, the dahlias
she drowned all summer in green fisted
devotion, her blue bowls
that cupped Asia in their palms
later all the black walls
the multiplying black walls
she painted late night
high up on the stepladder with
her chain lit cigarette version
of paradise
burning?

ALISON TOWNSEND

With No Words to Name This

I do not think my father meant wrong,
those first raw weeks after my mother's death,
when he took me, weeping,
into their bed, and held me,
shaking, while the whole house slept,
wrapped in its navy blue blankets
of grief and exhaustion.

I think he meant well,
meant to soothe the way
my mother had, her soft, powder-
scented body curving around me
when I was sick or scared.
I cannot remember
if he pressed his face
to my flat chest
where the nipples floated,
hard as unripe grapes.

Or if he touched me
in that cleft of darkness,
my small black sea heaving
against the arch of pubic bone.
I do not even know if he held me
against his own hardness,
or if he only held me,
and what I almost remember
is a story I have invented
to explain away a dream,
my body a knot of wet rope
only a mother's hands
could untangle.

ALISON TOWNSEND

Magic 8

My father gave it to my sister
one year for her ninth birthday.
But sometimes, when no one
was around I'd slip
into her room and ask
the Magic 8 questions,
tilting the black ball
back and forth in my hands
until an answer floated into
the porthole window at the top,
white words on a blue triangle,
rising from depths as black
as the Faber Castell ink
we used in eighth grade art.

The box it came in said
the ball was *to be used*
for entertainment purposes only.
But it was designed to answer
yes and no questions,
and so I asked them all,
admitting my secret hopes
as confidently as I imagined
Catholic kids did at confession.
And the oracle obliged,
responses swimming into focus
at my every request, though they
were never quite what I wanted
as I looked everywhere for signs
that I was normal, hoping
the ball would give me
answers like *It is certain*
or *All signs point to yes.*

No matter what I asked
the Magic 8 answered.
Would Bruce Colley
ask me to go steady?
Ask again later.
Would I really be grounded
the rest of the month?
It is decidedly so.
Might my parents give me
my own phone for Christmas?
My sources say no.

I always ran out of questions
in the end and sat there,
turning the ball over
and over in my hands as if
it was the witch's crystal
from *The Wizard of Oz*,
and I could see somewhere
far ahead in the future,
tiny figures full
of meaning running
toward me in the glass.

And still the answers
floated up, responding
as if by honest magic
to what I couldn't ask—
why my mother died young,
why my father remarried fast,
why looking out
my attic bedroom window
filled me with sadness—
as if the black ball
really knew more than I did,
stupid toy blinking open
and shut like an eye
that saw everything

(no stanza break)

and knew what life
was really about,
boiling it down to one
of the twenty possible answers:

Reply hazy.
Cannot predict now.
Concentrate and try again.

ANNA R. TREBORZE

Fog & Sheep

People regard me sadly.
Themselves,
the more so.
My strings get tangled.

I wave a tar
baby's rattle
at the thought-riddled
hordes, ivory-chained.

Peacocks grimace
from behind parrot cages.
Eyes are for thumb-
shutting, *Thank you.*

Flattery,
a wood lozenge,
a cure
for the murderous art.

(*Fun facts:* Our Father,
is art in heaven.
Just when you think:

you're done for.)

ANNA R. TREBORZE

Where You Go: I

Alone,

on the wavy-baked blacktop, Jesus

appears,

as he would to you if you were not so
concerned about that which makes you poorer. And it comes
    again:
that absent look in your face: attentiveless,
in your dimestore Lourdes.

In your face: is the face reaching out,
searching—
for the face you had
before Mommy & Daddy were born.

The face you long to love,
which longs to love you: face-to-face,
hanging onto the wall
above the Grand Canyon keychains
& pecan log rolls
in that Stuckeys,

we've just departed.

ARLENE TRIBBIA

Sure

I miss my brother sure
he drank Robitussin
washed down with beer
sure he smoked dope
& shot heroin
& went to prison
for selling to
an undercover cop

& sure he robbed
the town's only hot dog stand,
Gino's like I overheard
while I laid on my bed
staring up at the stars
under slanted curtains

& sure he used to
leave his two year old
son alone so he could
score on the street

but before all this
my brother sure
used to swing me up
onto his back, run
me around dizzy
through hallways and rooms
& we'd laugh & laugh
fall onto the bed finally
and he'd tickle me
to death sure

PETRA UHRIG

On Being an Immigrant, On Being a German-American

I'm perched atop a hyphen, sandwiched between two words,
two worlds, two languages. I'm munching on a piece
of Zwiebel bread.
This is where I live, how I feel
and think about everything, a dabbler, nibbler,
not a wholesale believer of anything. Once, I was six
years old in the middle of a meal in the middle of an ocean,
of a century.
It held a ladder and a choice of bread to eat.

But when did Tinkerbell usurp the Brothers Grimm? When did
Ich turn into *I* as if there were no other way of saying it?

Just after the Bay of Pigs and Cuban Missile Crisis, before a
stream
of assassinations, urban riots, anti-war demonstrations, a second
wave of feminism, there were smallpox vaccinations,
language lessons, new sweaters and socks, one suitcase
for each of us. My brother wore a shadow which our parents
did nothing about.

We sat at our restaurant table, floating,
buoyed somewhere between *Bitte* and *Thanks*,
steered toward the Statue of Liberty, when I asked,
"Wo ist mein Brot? Where's my bread?"
and my mother said, "On your plate."

That was it. The moment. Though my mother's face
tried to tamp any trace of it, her change-and-adjust,
don't-look-strange-or-foreign stare bearing down

(no stanza break)

on my sense of myself. We kept no hyphens on hand
like a packet of paper clips. You were
or you weren't. It was all or nothing. "Where?
I don't see it," I half-huffed, mustering rebellion,
because until that May day on a dash on the Atlantic,
a piece of bread was as recognizable as my hand-made
red wool winter coat and my thick black leggings.
I had trekked old cobbled streets in them, dodging hay carts,
trailing ancient, ubiquitous women. Bread women.
Well-crusted, well-kneaded, dressed in onions
and anise and caraway seeds. I almost fell off the edge

of the ship chasing porpoises showing off on the waves;
I felt a freedom deep breathing will grant in a manner no
language can duplicate. My seasick brother heaved his dinner
    again,
stomach empty, lungs tubercular
the day I looked around, over, right through
what I would later know as Wonder Bread. Blond edge,
soft belly, so mashed potatoey I thought it was part
of the plate. I sat on the edge of something other than
my seat, unaware of it. What was this I would sink
my teeth into? Graham crackers and milk, ketchup
and potato chips, schoolyard swings, regular showers.
When American kids yelled *Nazi!* at school,
I ran home to ask my mother what that meant.

PETRA UHRIG

In the End

as in the end of any ending
we walk away and stay
together. The moment,
thought, disperses and joins.
As forgotten as it is remembered.
And you thought each war
would be the war to end all wars. You
saw beginnings like a fool again.

The loose thread ripped from a seam
that won't scream on it's way to the carpet
is a hand lopped off at the wrist,
now aware of its sloppy existence.
We meet at different ends to discuss it.

But in the end, nothing cried, uttered,
begged for or against, lost or gained,
leaves its place, nor lingers. We're not talking
apocalypse, here. Just whispers in your ear
if you stop thinking a moment.

They say we're here, and when we're not here
we're bumping into others,
on the metro, at the mall. That's all.

Still scratching a phantom leg, you
say something new about closure; rub
an old purple lump on your skull,
deny the assault in light of another start,
unsure as a promise,
misleading as a photograph,
scar tissue stretched taut.

There is evil in the world, you say. But it doesn't sit
on your living room sofa smoking a joint
or reeking of armpit or waxing a spear; it asks
the right spelling of your name, repeats the five digits
of your zip code, knows which fork to use.

In the beginning we were fools. In the end,
we are fools to believe in beginnings.

SALLY VAN DOREN

The Plans

Construct a contour in the aftermath.
      It includes, of course,
the build-up, the prescient fore-
      knowledge, withheld from them,
of what was to pass.
              She knew,
      but could not articulate it,
except in her vigil, changing
      the plastic sheets wet with blood.
Others, doctors included, visited
      in reckless affirmation. Predictions
lagged behind the stealthy progress
      of the night thief.
              It happened
in his sleep, after either exhale or
      inhale. The rehab room carried
air from his wife and children.
      Pumped oxygen and breath
co-mingled in the mute countdown.
              Bound in the happening,
      they rallied, the parents pushing
hard on the trap door.
              They
did not know it was his last day. He spoke,
      smiled and lay in bed. He
forgot his birthdate, then he remembered it.
              He asked to take a nap and
he woke up from it.
              They did not hear
      the something coming to kill him.

MELISSA J. VARNAVAS

Mother's descent

Mother's angry tower descends

the basement stairs.

Spiders spin

dust and sunlight

from ceiling to floor.

She picks up the broom

and smiles.

In a swift movement, she begins

to sweep away the dust

but she leaves the spiders

for me.

REETIKA VAZIRANI

The Power of Darkness By Tolstoy

I turned twenty   years after Cleopatra
am cold post-war Stockholm's   widow I'll live in birds of
a migrant's eyes   photos seeing you looked at
lonely no I was fourteen a soaplather girl
man after beard whose father was I? in whose barn hat
circling four kroner a week and tips I made
the movies unmarried me enough faces of womens
planet Hitler loved   Anna Karenina
Greta Gustafsson 5'7" dark glasses Radha I spent
Garbo call me G.G. if love is beauty I am the window shopping
    for it

DAVID WAGONER

A Commencement Address (Short Version)

The world will say, "Make sense!"
Meaning it isn't enough
For you to taste, to listen,
To look around, to feel,
And to scent danger and love.

It will insist you learn
With whom and where and when
To be out of touch, to lose track,
To be tasteless, to turn a stone-
Deaf ear and a blind eye.

If, instead, you make no sense
At all to yourselves at first,
Remember it's an achievement
So far only your parents
And the rest of us have found

Sensible enough
To be worth living for.
Now here's a piece of paper
To hold, to gnaw, to crinkle,
To sniff at, and glance over.

DAVID WAGONER

Keep Out, Tresspassers Will Be Jailed After
They Get Out of the Hospitle, This Means You

The sign had worked so far: no other cars
Had beaten the grass down between the ruts,
And no one had stomped a path through the knee-high lawn
Lately or walked the plank up to the porch
And pushed the door on its only hinge but you.

Whatever could be wrenched or crowbarred loose
Had been, including the kitchen sink, and the floor
Was hanging tough by its linoleum.
In the living room, someone had built a fire
For hotdogs or heat, but not in the fireplace.

The holes gouged in the wallboard between studs
Went all the way to the woods, the holes in the ceiling
Went all the way to the sky, and the three holes
In the bathroom floor were offering
Indoor plumbing direct to the foundation.

You inspected the scene of the crime. A few remains
Of the biggest, longest, maybe the worst party
Ever. Three sticks of furniture. The last dishrag.
A tag end of a nightgown. In the bedroom,
No telling where the Beautyrest had been

Or why. You found some overdue grocery bills
And receipts for speeding fines. A note saying, *Baby*,

(no stanza break)

Gone to the dump again. You went outside.
A swing-set with no swings. A slide with no ladder.
And what comes down the chimney? Half the chimney.

Along the side path, blossoming in the sun,
Bright, everlasting slivers of windowpanes.
A trellis where the rose hadn't been wild
Enough to keep from choking on itself.
A wooden pump-tower, knock-kneed, straddling a well.

Over the barn door, a rusty horseshoe
Wrong side down.
Inside, some shotgun shells and barn owl pellets,
But the owls themselves no longer living aloft.
Underfoot, not enough straw for a scarecrow.

In the back yard, a tipped-over lawn chair,
No grimier than your jeans. You sat in it,
Neck deep in wavering grass, drinking your lunch
To celebrate all this picturesque failure.
It made you feel irrationally happy.

Being nosy and on your own, you'd crossed the threshold
With the diffident easy bluster of a landlord
Or a crooked building inspector or a burglar
Professional to the core or a case-worker
With a warrant or a tour guide casing a ruin.

You felt so self-contained, so worldly (and you
Still middle-aged) to see these premises
Vacated like the premises you'd made
About a wife and hypothetical family
Once upon a time on a model farm,

You went to the country tavern at sundown
And, under the influence of a jukebox
And other brilliant conversationalists,
Joined some familiar strangers out for a night:
Jocose, Bellicose, Lachrymose, Comatose.

317

DAVID WAGONER

The Three Monkeys

They sat there on my bookshelf, my first prize
    From a carnival, three plaster monkeys
        In a row. My father said they were See and Hear
And Speak No Evil and said to think
    Of what those three were doing
        As a kind of Sunday school, and so
I started to think. The one with his hands
    Over his eyes like a blindfold
        Could say whatever he felt like
And could hear what anyone said and forget it
    ᐧ Or remember. The one with his hands on his ears
        Had both eyes open
To everything going on and could say out loud
    Whatever he thought. The one clapping his mouth
        Shut could see and hear and keep in mind
Anything evil enough to reconsider
    Later, when those three, still stuck together
        But alone, could laugh and wave their hands in
  the air.

DAVID WAGONER

The Getaway

They had to act natural. They had to look like
      They were still parts of an ordinary day
            Together on the sidewalk across the street
To the unfamiliar car, yet they had to be
      Quick about it without running. They had to think
            Like themselves but look like other people
Taking those steps, remembering, knowing
      Every foot they could put between their bodies
            And the scene behind them, where the noise
Of buzzers and bells and yowling
      And terribly shocked voices was growing
            Louder and louder. They pulled away
As calmly as possible, staring straight ahead
      Straight-faced, not glancing once
            To either side or backward, let alone
At each other, and took a turn in the most unlikely
      Direction they could think of. Under the limit,
            They drove steadily, legally toward home.

ANNE WALDMAN

Again? (from *War Crime*)

Let's carry some industrial states in 2004
Let's carry our good old boys along
No flesh off our backs—
Let's be everything we want to be
Let's carry the worker-states—get those steel mills going again

Get those votes in Ohio
Pennsylvania
Let them off easy in
Turkey
Brazil
Russia

We need it
We need them working again
Working again, we do we do
We need them voting again, we do we do

It's a game, it's throbbing adrenaline game
Heart of steel, steel night
Steel in the vein
Turn on the war machines
USA thrum & motion

    on the move

NICOLE WALKER

Mistaking Doors for Windows

That was a good day. The day I thought only about money.
Not how much could I hide but how much could I borrow.

Forty-four friends of mine gave me cash. I didn't even write
Down how much. I just pocketed the crush and grime

And breathed hallelujah at them. Thank God they finally
Believed I had the touch and the face and the pockets.

In a red barroom I bought them all a drink—returned the favor
Met them head on, poured the beer, carried the glasses.

I took off my rings—laid them on the table—let everybody
Pick the one they liked the most the most. Later, in the parking
    lot

Head over fence, fence stopping me from moving forward
From letting go, from making my way out of town

With the money and the drinks and fingers free and wet
The fence wore its black rain like my father wore his coat

Like it didn't even notice. The damn fence gave me splinters
Let my face bleed, soaked up my spit. I think it took the money.

I went back in the morning to see if I had left the money
By the fence like one of those roadside memorials with their rose

Throws, petalling: I died here. In between fence and pavement
I found a book of matches. John's matches that he gave me last
    night

To burn the money. No wonder my hands stunk of sulphur
And the fingernails had turned yellow. I thought I was just
    turning

Into my father and old as a bookstore cat. Fur separating from
    bones
Bones into presses, my imprint cased in the smoky vinyl of a
    chair.

DANEEN WARDROP

The Political Unconscious

Dozens of slim men in fatigue greens, the banquet tent is fatigue green
this Ft. Bliss, Thanksgiving.
                    The Colonel's family
                              enters like a working fairy tale.

Combat boots white with shine.
Outside it snows tiny spurs. The Colonel is everyone's father.

The Colonel's wife might as well wear Jackie Kennedy gloves
                                        cut off at the wrist.
            Gripping purse strap, I, the Colonel's daughter, leave a scar
        of even stitches across my palm.

History is what hurts.

The men look at the Colonel.
The men and the daughter don't look at each other, someone
            would court martial someone right there on the floor.

The men will train, they'll turn tanks, go somewhere located in a TV.

                    Coughing a secular prayer,
        the Colonel asks that something bless the loved ones far away,
                        that something big as the desert bless the loved
        ones far away.

All the bodies sway in place,
poised in something big as the desert.

All this soft canteen food,
all these teeth.

ELLEN WEHLE

Like the Green Bay Tree

Rest assured, the wicked will flourish. Bus drivers who see you running
to their stop will step on the gas. Liars win trips to Hawaii. The woman

stealing office supplies heads Personnel and refuses to give you the job.
Smallness shall be king. Acts of kindness given no more weight than air

and sloth, rapacity—a host of sins, gargoyle-faced—endlessly rewarded.
What is this world but a droplet of water, spinning in the sightless dark?

Behind venetian blinds, your neighbors watch the ambulance pull up, no
lights flashing: they wonder *Should we...?* and take another sip of coffee.

Whose roots are slender, gossamer-fine. All-encroaching. Strong as
    iron.

MIKE WHITE

Bird

The brain sick bird
has drawn a small crowd.

On the sidewalk, unafraid
of passing feet, the bird pivots
and turns and turns, unsteady
wings outstretched
in some old dream of flight.

On and on without end or interruption
until someone gasps out laughing.

CATHERINE WING

Beauty: To Do

10:00, 3:00, 7:00, feed the dragon.
Practice happy face, smile, no ugh.
Please march, as the drum bangs on.

For the garden, salt on the slugs
And only Sundays to slack off.
Be, Beauty, Be! Don't lurk.

Remember B-12 for agony,
B-6 and C in case of heart ruckus.
Don't mention 100 years slumber, the rape, again.

Wipe your feet after trekking in briar muck.
Catch up with your lag.
Find a way to revitalize your tired luck.

Be charming to guests until they are gone.
In case of a fire, call for a fire truck.
When the Prince is around, make sure to be on.

CATHERINE WING

In Reverse

Here the moon plays catapult to cow.
The sky rewinds its batting back
To the horizon. Here it's Jill and Jack.

Here the clouds zip up the rain
And a ripple forms a raindrop.
We down hiccups. We swallow the baby.

Here a moth is born from fire
And it's the face that slaps down the hand.
Spins down the church from the spire.

Here dynamite rouses the rubble
And a pinwheel pulls on the wind.
A clown inhales the bubbles

While the Piper—Pied—scatters
The children. And those who have died
Back pedal into life and matter

Greatly to the rest of us. Here
Where we take back our kisses
And pocket our handshakes.
Here where we edit the tide.

JONAH WINTER

The Fool in Shakespeare

Amongst Shakespeare's works, many works
contains The Fool. The Fool
appears on over 18 works
by Shakespeare. Shakespeare
utilizes The Fool to underscore
human frailty. He reiterates
this in several of his works
in which The Fool re-appears.
Similarly, one of the things
we see in Shakespeare
is a thing
called "*foolishness*." "Foolishness"
occurs in several passages
involving "The Fool." "The Fool"
enters into the scenes
where The Fool is called for.
Therefore, Shakespeare
uses The Fool
throughout his countless works.
These novels ensconce the need
for many things, including
The Fool, "foolishness,"
characters who are not The Fool,
and Hamblet.
In conclusion,
"foolishness" is a thing
created by The Fool
(in Shakespeare).

JONAH WINTER

Escape from the Looking-Glass

Last seen bounding over rooftops,
having scarred the veterinarian for life…
probably in Montana, or north,
probably safe inside some blizzard,
slumped across a bar
livin' out some old Hank Williams song,
too drunk to hear it's all in his head: *How,*
if this was supposed to be the Here and Now,
no baggage, no return stubs,
how come the pool balls
sound so far away?
Who are all these strangers
from another century?
Why are they here, in their old-style clothes?
And the strangest one of all, there in the mirror—
why the paws instead of hands?
It's getting darker.
The fan is getting louder.
Everything's an icon:
the barmaid's smile,
petrified, detached
from the caribou sky
and the white flowers of last year
and the year before that,
yet another Hollywood façade
[slow fade to indigo
and limitless stars]…

in the beginning, God made… Perhaps we
can make a religion
of surfaces. Perhaps these Cheshire eyes and whiskers
is all there is. Perhaps this fur

(no stanza break)

329

is the last frontier, these padded feet
still numb from the cold,
too tired to move
one claw. Perhaps I
am That.

AMANDA KATERI WISNIEWSKI

Making Lipstick

"Nothing in the world is accomplished without passion"—fortune cookie

Take a penis.
Cut its tip
at a comfortable angle
and let the blood
spiral down, fill in
the rigid inches
of overused flesh
so that it is red,
smooth,
attractive to men.
Coat it with glistening
wax, and stick it
in a tube that allows
a girl
to determine its proper length,
as she applies it
to another set of angry lips,
reminding herself
what her dirty mouth is for.

JOSEPH P. WOOD

Supreme Court Makes Pact to Lose Virginity by the End of December 2002

We were so busy making laws we forgot to make
it with each other. Our black robes blackened
the fire smoldering in our loins. That changed

when all those jock Senators, the football players
who often cartwheeled the cheerleaders,
tossed eggs in our direction & started to guffaw.

How little we were, shot down off our marble
podiums; we once stood above the country
like a ranger on fire look out. And for what save

your nights when the fathers step from the adult
bookstores blinking their filth like a promise,
& when the mothers rock themselves to sleep.

When you see us towering over the news
correspondents, redwoods stretching toward
the sun like your hearts, think of us asking

each other *what's that on your soda can*;
it looks like a hair, but these days we see
anything to appear less alone.

LAURA WRIGHT

out the window, cleveland looms overhead

the air is caked
with citrus vanilla and asphalt
in our department-store kitchen,
august 18.
dinosaurs are resurfacing the road,
which is fine with me—
roars and flutes
make summer worthwhile,
cutting up fruit, baking.

this is our little square
of the suburban periodic table:
pink t-shirt and ripped-up jeans,
pizza coupons and all lowercase letters.
cloudy and clear ice cubes
sail the dog's water.

sounds obscuring conversation—
I know there's sidewalk chalk
somewhere in my closet.
too warm to bake,
arm around waist,
good thing the windows
float open for us.

ABU BAKR, c.570-634, was the Prophet Mohammed's closest companion and adviser, and first convert to Islam. His prominence in the community was enhanced by Mohammed's marriage to his daughter A'ishah and also when Abu Bakr was the prophet's companion on the journey to Medina in 622. After Mohammed died (632), an assembly of Moslems in Mecca elected Abu Bakr as the first 'khalifat rasul Allah' (successor of the Prophet of God), or caliph.

DICK ALLEN is the author of seven collections of poetry, including his newest, *The Day Before: New Poems*, published by Sarabande Books in April, 2003. He has poems recently published or forthcoming in *The Atlantic Monthly*, *The Gettysburg Review*, *Smartish Pace*, *The Edge City Review*, as well as the anthologies *Contemporary American Poetry: Behind the Scenes* and *The Poetry Anthology, 1912-2002*. In 2001, he took early retirement from college teaching in order to "live simply and devote myself completely to poetry."

ERIC ANDERSON's poems are forthcoming in *Prairie Schooner*, *Rattle*, *Sentence*, and the *Seneca Review*. His first chapbook, *Confederate Season*, was published in 2002. On Monday nights, he bowls in Lorain, OH.

SHERI ANDERSON is a poet. After a small midlife crisis (way too much focus on her paying job), she is tiptoeing back into the writing world. She currently resides in San Antonio, Texas, with her husband, son and stepson.

JULIANNA BAGGOTT's collection of poems, *This Country of Mothers*, was published by SIU Press in 2001. Her poetry has appeared widely in publications including: *Poetry*, *Best American Poetry 2000*, and *Ms. Magazine*. She is the author of two best-selling novels, *Girl Talk* (2001) and *The Miss American Family* (2002). A new novel, *The Madam*, is forthcoming.

JEFFERY BAHR lives in Colorado and has work published or upcoming in a variety of publications, including *The Alaska Quarterly Review*, *Barrow Street*, *Black Warrior*, *Chelsea*, *Indiana Review*, *The Journal*, *Many Mountains Moving*, *Notre Dame Review*, *Prairie Schooner* and *Quarterly West*.

THERESA DEVINE BANFORD is currently finishing her first manuscript, tentatively titled *Close to Home*. She lives in New Jersey with her husband and two daughters.

J. T. BARBARESE's poem, "Boy on His Father's Shoulders", is included in the author's most recent collection: *A Very Small World*, new from Orchises Press. Recently published (University of Pennsylvania, 1999) is his translation of *Children of Herakles*.

HADARA BAR-NADAV's recent publications appear or are forthcoming in *Laurel Review*, *Passages North*, *Spoon River Poetry Review*, *Northwest Review*, *Malahat Review*, *Pleiades*, *Prairie Schooner*, *West Branch*, *Southeast Review*, *Chattahoochee Review*, *Water~Stone*, *Poet Lore*, and other journals. Currently pursuing her PhD in creative writing, she teaches in the English department at the University of Nebraska—Lincoln, and is also on the editorial staff of *Prairie Schooner*.

WALTER BARGEN's ninth book of poetry is *The Body of Water* published by Timberline Press in 2003. His poems appear in *Iowa Review*, *Boulevard*, *Beloit Poetry Journal*, *Notre Dame Review*, and *New Letters*. www.walterbargen.com

COLEMAN BARKS has spent twenty-seven years working with Persian scholars to bring Rumi's poetry into American English: *The Essential Rumi*, *The Soul of Rumi*, and *RUMI: The Book of Love* from Harper San Francisco. Recent volumes of his own poetry are *Tentmaking* and *Club: Granddaughter Poems* from Maypop. He has retired from university teaching. He lives in Athens, GA.

TONY BARNSTONE is Associate Professor of English at Whittier College, the author of a book of poetry, *Impure* (University Press of Florida, 1999) and a chapbook of poems, *Naked Magic* (Mainstreet Rag, 2002). He has edited and/or translated several books of Chinese poetry and prose. His forthcoming book is *The Anchor Book of Chinese Poetry* (Anchor Books, 2004).

STEVEN BARZA is Director of Creative Writing at the University of Richmond and the author of the chapbook Man Overboard (Finishing Line Press, 2002). His poems have appeared in *Poetry*, *Ascent*, *New Letters*, *Utne*, *California Quarterly*, and *Wisconsin Review*, among others.

AMY BEEDER was a Bread Loaf Scholar in 2002 and won a "Discovery"/The Nation Award in 2001. Her poems are forthcoming in *Prairie Schooner*, *Pleiades* and *Connecticut Review*. She is Poetry Editor of *Blue Mesa Review*.

AARON BELZ is a member of the faculty of St. Louis University. He holds a Ph.D. in English Literature. His poems have appeared in *88*, *Boston Review*, *Fine Madness*, *Fence*, and many other periodicals.

F. J. BERGMANN is from Wisconsin. She illustrates zoonoses and maintains various websites including madpoetry.org. She received the 2003 Mary Roberts Rinehart national poetry award, and has a chapbook, *Sauce Robert*, forthcoming from Pavement Saw Press.

EDWARD BOCCIA, painter and poet, was born in Newark, New Jersey in 1921. He is Professor Emeritus, School of Fine Arts, Washington University, St. Louis, MO. His paintings are in public and private collections in the U.S., Europe and South America. He is the author of four collections of poetry.

DEBORAH BOGEN's chapbook, *Living by the Children's Cemetary* won the 2002 ByLine Press competition. Her work has appeared in *Field, Poetry International, Iron Horse Literary Review, JAMA, Mudfish, Poet Lore* and *Rivendell*, among others. Her book-length manuscript, *Landscape with Silos*, is in search of a publisher.

GERRY BOLAND was born in Dublin in 1954 and now lives in north Roscommon. He is working on his first collection of poems, *Ahimsa* (harmless to all living things). He is currently writing the second volume of his children's trilogy, *Tales of Saliman*.

SUSAN BRENNAN is currently a graduate student at NYU Creative Writing program in Poetry. She has taught creative writing as an adjunct teacher at NYU and as an assistant teacher for at-risk students with Community Word Project at PS 132, Bronx, NY. She recently attended the Squaw Valley Writer's Community and has organized poetry readings throughout New York City. Susan is also a performer and yoga teacher.

drea brown is a native of St. Louis. She holds a BA in creative writing and poetics from Hollins University in Roanoke, VA. Her work has appeared in various journals and anthologies.

ASHLEY CAPPS received her M.A. in English from Ohio University in 2002. She was the Jay C. and Ruth Halls Poetry Fellow at the Wisconsin Writers Institute for 2002-'03.

ALAN CATLIN has been making the poetry scene in the "littles" and "not so littles" since the middle seventies. His latest book is a selected poems from Pavement Saw Press titled *Drunk and Disorderly*. Forthcoming is a chapbook from Pudding Publications, *The Last Bus from Albany*, describing commuting in ways that have never been used before.

BARBARA DILTZ CHANDLER has worked as a journalist, librarian, hospice caregiver and failed chicken farmer. Her photographs and poetry have appeared in *Petroglyph*, *Manzanita* and *Whetstone*, among other publications. Her book on avalanche safety was published by Signpost Books.

JAN CLAUSEN was born and raised in the Pacific Northwest. For the last several decades she has made her life in Brooklyn. She is a NYFA poetry fellow in 2003. Her latest book is a memoir, *Apples and Oranges* (Houghton Mifflin, 1999). She has published three books of fiction and was awarded an NEA fiction fellowship. Poems have recently appeared in *Luna*, *Ploughshares* and *XConnect*.

DAVID CLEWELL's poem in this issue is included in his newest collection—*The Low End of Higher Things*—just published this summer by the University of Wisconsin Press. Clewell is also the author of two booklength poems—*The Conspiracy Quartet* and *Jack Ruby's America* (Garlic Press)—and several other collections.

SCOTT COFFEL's poetry appeared in *Margie*'s inaugural issue and was nominated for a Pushcart Prize. His work has been published in *Salmagundi*, *The Paris Review*, *Ploughshares*, *Antioch Review*, *Prairie Schooner*, and elsewhere.

CAROLE COHEN resides as a liberal in St. Louis, MO. and was Senior Editor of *Boulevard* literary magazine. Her poems have appeared in *Ascent*, *The Sou'wester*, *The Cape Rock*, *The Midwest Quarterly*, *The Spoon River Poetry Review*, *The Madison Review* and many others. Her work has also appeared in several anthologies.

ROBERT CORDING is the author of four volumes of poetry: *Lifelist* (winner of the Ohio State University Press Prize, 1987); *What Binds Us To This World* (Copper Beach, 1991); *Heavy Grace* (Alice James, 1996) and, most recently, *Against Consolation* (CavanKerry, 2002). New work is forthcoming in *Paris Review*, *Sewanee Review*, *Southern Review*, *DoubleTake*, *Georgia Review*, and elsewhere. He teaches at the College of the Holy Cross in Worcester, MA.

ANN CROSSMAN currently lives in Seoul, Korea with her husband and is tinkering with her second manuscript, inspired by kimchi.

CARL DENNIS is the author of eight books of poetry including, most recently, *Practical Gods*, which was awarded in 2002 the Pulitzer Prize in Poetry. A recipient of fellowships from the Guggenheim Foundation and the National Endowment for the Arts, in 2000 he received the Ruth

Lilly Prize from *Poetry Magazine* and the Modern Poetry Association for his contribution to American poetry. He is Artist in Residence at the State University of New York at Buffalo, and is a sometime member of the faculty of the M.F.A. program in creative writing at Warren Wilson College.

CATHERINE DOTY was born and grew up in Paterson, New Jersey. She attended the University of Iowa while working as a cook, cartoonist, waitress and bartender, and has long worked as a poet-in-residence in many, many schools. She lives in New York City.

DENISE DUHAMEL's most recent poetry collection is *Queen for a Day: Selected and New Poems* (University of Pittsburgh Press, 2001). A winner of a National Endowment for the Arts Fellowship, she teaches at Florida International University in Miami. Her work has been included in recent issues of *TriQuarterly*, *Ploughshares*, and *Denver Quarterly*.

RUSSELL EDSON was born in Connecticut in 1935. Mr. Edson is the author of eleven books of poetry including most recently, *The Wounded Breakfast* and *The Tunnel: Selected Poems*. He is regarded as America's most gifted prose poet.

DAN ENCARNACION has recently received an M.F.A. in writing from the California College of Arts and Crafts. He is a native and continuing resident of the Oakland/San Francisco Bay Area. Dan has previously been published in *The Peralta Press*.

RHINA P. ESPAILLAT is a Dominican-born bilingual poet with five books to her credit, most recently *Where Horizons Go* and *Rehearsing Absence*, winners, respectively, of the 1998 T. S. Eliot Prize for Poetry and the 2001 Richard Wilbur Award. Her next two books are due out later this year and in spring 2004, as winners of the National Poetry Book Award sponsored by Salmon Run Press, and the Stanzas Prize sponsored by David Robert Books. Espaillat lives in Newburyport, MA with her sculptor husband, Alfred Moskowitz.

SUSAN FAIRFIELD has taught comparative literature and published papers on Greek and Latin poetry. A trained psychoanalyst, she has also written on psychoanalysis and postmodernism. In addition to her clinical practice, she now works as an editor and translator.

MELANIE FIGG has poems in *The Iowa Review*, *Mid-American Review*, *Crab Orchard Review* and other journals. Her manuscript, *Lucky Bird*, was a finalist for the 2003 Agnes Starrett Lynch Poetry Prize from the University of Pittsburgh. She has won many awards including a Loft

McKnight Award and a Jerome Fellowship. She received her MFA from the University of Utah in 1999 where she was the poetry editor of *Quarterly West* for three years.

SUSAN FIRER's two most recent books of poems are *The Laugh We Make When We Fall*, winner of 2001 Backwaters Prize and *The Lives of the Saints and Everything*, winner of the Cleveland State Poetry Center Prize and Posner Award. She lives, writes, and works along the western shore of Lake Michigan.

MAXWELL FOX reports that "Js" represents his first poem in publication. It was composed to explain the experience of his mother. Originally, the poem was created in seven parts, one for each of his mother's children.

ALICE FRIMAN has new work in *Poetry*, *The Georgia Review*, *Prairie Schooner*, *Boulevard* and others. Her latest book, *Zoo*, U of Arkansas Press, 1999, won the Ezra Pound Poetry Award from Truman State University and the Sheila Motton Prize from the New England Poetry Club. She is a recipient of a Creative Renewal Fellowship from the Arts Council of Indianapolis and the winner of the 2001 James Boatwright Prize from *Shenandoah*.

PATRICIA L. FRISELLA has won accolades for her essays, short stories, and creative nonfiction, but poetry is where her passion lies, and where she expends most of her creativity. She believes in poetry's power to transform and save.

FRANK GIAMPIETRO's poem "The Afterlife" is nominated for a 2003 Pushcart Prize. He is a contributing editor to *Hunger Mountain: the Vermont College Journal of Arts and Letters*. His work appears or is forthcoming in *Barrow Street*, *Tulane Review*, *Diner*, and elsewhere.

ROBERT GIBB's new book, *The Burning World*, will be available in 2004.

DEBRA GINGERICH received her M.F.A. in Writing from Vermont College of Union Institute and University. Her poetry has been published in *The Circle Magazine*, *DreamSeeker Magazine* and *The Mennonite*. She lives in Philadelphia, PA where she works as a communications coordinator.

JAMES STONE GOODMAN (Hebrew Union College, '81) serves as rabbi to Neve Shalom Congregation and the Central Reform Congregation in St. Louis, Missouri. Rabbi Goodman founded *Shalvah*, (which means serenity in Hebrew), an outreach arm of Congregation Neve Shalom, to assist those struggling with addiction. "Blessing" is his first published poem.

DEBORA GREGER is the author of *Desert Fathers, Uranium Daughters* (Penguin, 1996). Her poetry has appeared in *The New Yorker*, *The New York Times*, *The Nation*, *New Republic*, *Yale Review*, and *The Norton Anthology of Poetry* (1996). She teaches at the University of Florida at Gainesville.

JOHN GREY is an Australian born poet, playwright, and musician who has lived in the US since the late seventies. His work has recently appeared in *South Carolina Review*, *Confluence*, *Sojourn*, and *Small Town Rain* with more work forthcoming in *Pennsylvania English*, *Bogg*, and *Louisiana Review*. Mr. Grey is the winner of the 1998 Rhysling award for Science Fiction Poetry.

FIONA GRIMSHAW is a native of Northern Ireland. She studied poetry at Princeton University under Jean Hollander. She lives with her husband and three grown daughters in St. Louis, MO.

PIOTR GWIAZDA's poetry has been featured in *Columbia: A Journal of Literature & Art*, *The Southern Review*, and *Washington Square*. New work is forthcoming in *Barrow Street* and *Hotel Amerika*. Mr. Gwiazda's book reviews appear in the *Times Literary Supplement* and *Black Warrior Review*. His manuscript, *Gagarin Street*, was a finalist in this year's Lena-Miles Wever Todd Poetry Series Book Prize (Pleiades/LSU Press).

JOHN HAINES' most recent book of poems, *For the Century's End, Poems 1990-99*, was published by the University of Washington Press in 2001. In spring 2001 he was Poet-in-Residence at the Stadler Center, Bucknell University. He has most recently returned to Alaska as Northern Momentum Scholar at the University of Alaska Fairbanks, spring 2003. He has a new collection of essays and reviews in preparation.

JAMES HAUG's most recent book, *Walking Liberty*, won the Morse Poetry Prize and was published by Northeastern University Press. He's published one other collection, *The Stolen Car*, and a chapbook, *Fox Luck*.

CAROLINE HEMPHILL's poems appear or are forthcoming in *Black Warrior Review*, *Graham House Review*, *Green Mountains Review* and *Phoebe*. She recently received an Illinois Arts Council fellowship in poetry.

WILLIAM HEYEN is the author of *Erika: Poems of the Holocaust, Pterodactyl Rose, Ribbons: The Gulf War, Crazy Horse in Stillness* (winner in 1997 of the Small Press Book Award), and numerous other volumes of poetry. He recently edited *September 11, 2001: American Writers Respond* for The Etruscan Press. He lives in Bridgeport, NY.

JANE HIRSHFIELD is the author of five collections of poetry: *Given Sugar, Given Salt* (finalist for the 2001 National Book Critics Circle Award, and winner of the Bay Area Book Reviewers Award), *The Lives of the Heart, The October Palace, Of Gravity & Angels,* and *Alaya,* as well as a book of essays on poetry, *Nine Gates.* Her other honors include fellowships from the Guggenheim and Rockefeller Foundations. Hirshfield's work has appeared in *The New Yorker, The Atlantic, The Nation, The American Poetry Review, Best American Poetry,* and many other publications.

JOHN HODGEN's *In My Father's House* (1993) won the Bluestem Award from Emporia State University, and his second book *Bread Without Sorrow* (2001) won the Balcones Poetry Prize from Austin Community College. Hodgen used to dig graves, but now teaches writing at Assumption College.

CYNTHIA MARIE HOFFMAN is the founding editor of *Frantic Egg,* a mini-journal of poetry. She tied for first place for the 2002 Mary Roberts Rinehart Award and is the winner of the Virginia Downs Poetry Award of the same year. Her work has appeared in such journals as *Poet Lore, Gargoyle, Phoebe, Rattapallax,* and *Rattle.* Cynthia is an M.F.A. candidate in Poetry at George Mason University, where she teaches English on fellowship.

HILARY HOLLADAY is Associate Professor of Literature at the University of Massachusetts-Lowell. She is the author of *Ann Petry* (Twayne, 1996) and *Wild Blessings: The Poetry of Lucille Clifton* (LSU Press, forthcoming).

KARLA M. HUSTON is the author of *A Halo of Watchful Eyes* (Wolf Angel Press, 1997) and *Pencil Test* (Cassandra Press, 2001). She recently earned her MA in English from the University of Wisconsin Oshkosh. She has published poems and reviews in many literary journals.

HOLLY IGLESIAS' work has appeared in *Prairie Schooner, Arts & Letters, The Prose Poem, The Massachusetts Review* and *U.S. Latino Review.* She was awarded an individual artist grant for poetry by the Massachusetts Cultural Council in 2000, as well as the Frank O'Hara Award from Thorngate Road Press for her chapbook, *Good Long Enough.*

Her collection of prose poems, *Hands-On Saints*, was recently released from Quale Press. She lives in western Massachusetts where she coordinates a middle-school peer mediation program.

COLETTE INEZ has authored eight collections of poetry, the most recent of which is *Clemency* from Carnegie Mellon University Press. She has received fellowships from the Guggenheim and Rockefeller Foundations, and twice from the NEA. A visiting professor at Cornell, Ohio, Bucknell and Colgate Universities, she has been on the faculty of Columbia University's Undergraduate Writing Program since 1983. *The Way Home; The Poetry of Colette Inez*, Word Press, Cincinnati, Ohio is new in 2003.

ANNE WARD JAMIESON has held a variety of day jobs including writing grant proposals, selling books, and teaching, but remains, above all, a constant student. Her poems have appeared (or soon will) in *The North American Review*, *Confrontation*, *5 AM*, *The MacGuffin*, *The Texas Review*, and elsewhere.

TROY JOLLIMORE's poetry has been published in various journals including *Ploughshares*, *Press*, and *The Cider Press Review*. He makes his second appearance in *Margie*.

ALLISON JOSEPH lives and teaches in Carbondale, Illinois, where she is on the faculty of Southern Illinois University, edits *Crab Orchard Review*, and directs the Young Writers Workshop. Her most recent book is *Imitation of Life* (Carnagie Mellon.) She won the 2003 Word Press Poetry Prize for her next book, *Worldly Pleasures*, forthcoming in 2004.

EVE JOSEPH has published work in various Canadian journals, including *Grain*, *Malahat* and *Vintage*. She is a counselor at Victoria Hospice and lives in Brentwood Bay with her family.

JESSE LEE KERCHEVAL is the author of six books, including the poetry collection, *World as Dictionary* and *Space*, a memoir about growing up in Florida during the moon race. Her second poetry collection, *Dog Angel*, is forthcoming from the University of Pittsburg Press. She is the Sally Meade Hands Professor of English at the University of Wisconsin-Madison where she directs both the Wisconsin Institute for Creative Writing and their new M.F.A. program.

ROBERT KING is a Professor Emeritus from the University of North Dakota and currently lectures at the University of Northern Colorado. His poetry has recently been published in *Poetry* and is forthcoming in

Missouri Review and *Atlanta Review*. Mr. King's latest chapbook, *Naming Names*, appeared in 2001 from Palanquin Press.

KARI LYNNE KINKELE lives in Cincinnati, OH. She is an artist continuing her studies. *Margie* is pleased to present her first publication of poetry.

DAVID KIRBY is the Robert O. Lawton Distinguished Professor of English at Florida State University. In 2003 he received a fellowship from the John Simon Guggenheim Memorial Foundation. He is the author or co-author of twenty-two books. His work appears in the *Best American Poetry* and *Pushcart Prize* series. A recent poetry collection, *The House of Blue Light*, was published in LSU Press's Southern Messenger series, which will also publish his forthcoming book, *The Ha-Ha*.

SHERRYL KLEINMAN is a professor in the Department of Sociology at the University of North Carolina, Chapel Hill. She has published creative nonfiction and poetry in *Iris*, *Rosebud*, *The Independent*, *The Sun*, and other venues.

TED KOOSER is a retired life insurance company executive who lives in rural Nebraska. His most recent book, a memoir entitled *Local Wonders; Seasons in the Bohemian Alps*, has just been published by University of Nebraska Press. Forthcoming next spring from Copper Canyon Press is *Braided Creek*, a collaboration in poetry with Jim Harrison.

RAPHAEL KOSEK lives with her family in the Hudson Valley. She is a Vassar graduate and has recently published poems in *Water-Stone*, *Kalliope*, and the *Potomac Review*. She is a '99 recipient of a New York Arts Council grant, and is currently working on a book of poems inspired by Georgia O'Keefe's paintings.

DAVID KRESH has three collections of poetry, including *Tell Me* (BOA Editions), which was a finalist for the National Book Award. He recently co-edited an anthology of writing on tattoos, *Dorothy Parker's Elbow*, due from Warner in October 2002.

MAXINE KUMIN is the author of 13 books of poetry, most recently *The Long Marriage*, as well as *Always Beginning: Essays on a Life in Poetry* and a memoir, *Inside the Halo and Beyond*. She and her husband live on a farm in New Hampshire.

DANIEL J. LANGTON was born in Paterson and raised in Harlem. He attended St. Paul's and Hayes as a scholarship boy. His work has appeared in *Poetry, The Atlantic, The Nation, The Paris Review* and *Iowa Review.* Mr. Langton's, *QUERENCIA,* won the Devins Award from *Missouri Review.* His most recent book is *LIFE FORMS.*

LOY LEDBETTER is a retired executive from Ralston Purina Company. He is currently President of the St. Louis Poetry Center and has been involved in the St. Louis poetry community for many years. He is also a creative photographer.

STELLASUE LEE is the author of *Crossing the Double Yellow Line, After I Fall, Over to You* and *13 Los Angeles Poets,* the ONTHEBUS Poets Series Number One (Bombshelter Press). Lee teaches privately, as well as at writers' conferences. She is the editor of the literary journal *RATTLE.*

GARY LEISING recently received a Ph.D. in English from the University of Cincinnati. His poems have appeared recently in *Quarterly West, Blackbird,* and the *Sewanee Theological Review.* He will begin teaching English at Northern Kentucky University in the fall.

RODNEY TERICH LEONARD is a poet, lecturer and curator. He is also a graduate of New School University whose research interests include female vocalists, particularly Nina Simone and Nancy Wilson. Mr. Leonard is also the founder of the Harlem Artist Salon, a salon series showcasing the talent of emerging and established artists and scholars.

DANIEL H. LIGHTSEY is a 66-year-old fugitive from the bastions of the counter culture; a trophy of grace; and an award winning poet. He resides in Joppa, Maryland with his wife, Sandra.

ELLINE LIPKIN is completing a Ph.D. in Creative Writing and Literature at the University of Houston. She received her M.F.A. in poetry from Columbia University. She has work forthcoming in *The Poets Grimm,* to be published by Story Line Press in 2003.

DUANE LOCKE, Doctor of Philosophy in English Renaissance literature, Professor Emeritus of the Humanities, was Poet in Residence at the University of Tampa for over 20 years. He has had over 2,000 of his own poems published in such periodicals as *American Poetry Review, The Nation, Literary Quarterly, Black Moon,* and *Bitter Oleander.* He is the author of fourteen volumes of poetry.

A. LOUDERMILK's poetry collection *The Daughterliest Son* is available from Swan Scythe Press. Poetry and essays have appeared in *Tin House,*

Mississippi Review, *Cream City Review*, *River Teeth*, *Journal of Consumer Culture*, *Journal X*, and elsewhere. He teaches at Indiana University.

GEORGE LOONEY's *Attendant Ghosts* is available from Cleveland State University Press (2000). *Animals Housed in the Pleasure of Flesh* won the 1995 Bluestein Award and was published by Bluestein Press. His poems have appeared in *The Kenyon Review*, *New England Review*, *Quarterly West*, *Prairie Schooner*, *The Gettysburg Review*, and elsewhere. Mr. Looney received a National Endowment for the Arts Fellowship for his poetry.

ALICE LYONS was born in Patterson, New Jersey and now lives in County Roscommon, Ireland. In 2002, she received the Patrick Kavanagh Award for her first collection of poems entitled *Speck*.

ELIZABETH MARSH is a junior at Saint Louis University, whose passion for writing was fueled by an English teacher at a young age. Inspiration for *Beyond Gender* came from observations made at Union Station in Chicago.

TRAPETA B. MAYSON, 35, native of Liberia, immigrated to the USA in 1975. She lives in Philadelphia. Trapeta is a 2002 Pew Fellow in the Arts as well as 2000 PA Council on the Arts Fellow. She is a social worker and also works with young people in the arts based after school programs.

SHARA McCALLUM is the author of two books of poetry, *The Water Between Us* and *Song of Thieves* (University of Pittsburgh Press, 1999, 2003). McCallum teaches and directs the Stadler Center for Poetry at Bucknell University in Pennsylvania.

KATHLEEN McGOOKEY's first book, *Whatever Shines*, is available from White Pine Press. Her poetry has appeared or is forthcoming in *Boston Review*, *Passages North*, *Ploughshares*, *Quarterly West*, *Verse*, *Willow Springs*, and many other periodicals. Her poems are also presented in a number of anthologies, including: *The Party Train: An Anthology of North American Prose Poetry* (New Rivers Press, 1995).

RENNIE McQUILKIN's poems have been published in *The Atlantic*, *Poetry*, *The Southern Review*, *Crazyhorse*, *The Gettysburg Review*, *The Yale Review*, *Chelsea*, *The Hudson Review*, *The Southwest Review*, *The North American Review*, *The Ontario Review*, and other journals and magazines. He has new work forthcoming in *Poetry* and *The American Scholar*. His awards include fellowships from the NEA and the Connecticut Commission on the Arts. He recently directed the Sunken Garden Poetry Festival in Farmington, CT.

PETER MEINKE's most recent collections are *Zinc Fingers* (2000) and *Scars* (1996), both in the Pitt Poetry Series. He has recently been appointed to the Darden Endowed Chair in Creative Writing at Old Dominion University, Norfolk, VA.

BILL MEISSNER is Director of Creative Writing at St. Cloud State University in Minnesota. His books of poetry are: *Learning to Breathe Underwater* and *The Sleepwalker's Son* (both from Ohio U. Press) and *Twin Sons of Different Mirrors* (Milkweed Editions). His book of short stories is *Hitting Into the Wind* (Random House Hardcover/SMU Press Paperback). He plays basketball occasionally at a fitness club, but has never made a half-court shot.

MARIO MILOSEVIC has placed poems in *The Black Warrior Review*, *Chase Park*, *Nerve Cowboy*, *Pearl*, *Rattle*, and many others within the past two years. He works in a small town library in Bigfoot country on the banks of the Columbia River.

SUSANNA MISHLER is an MFA student of poetry at the University of Arizona, where she is a poetry editor for Sonora Review. She has work forthcoming in Spoon River. Her permanent home is Anchorage, Alaska.

MICHAEL MOTT, whose work appeared in the first volume of *Margie*, has published four novels, an award-winning biography of Thomas Merton, and six collections of poetry, including his *Woman and the Sea: Selected Poems* (Anhinga Press). He is working on a group of poems that match incidents in a childhood on the eve of the Second World War to the drawings and paintings of the insane artist Richard Dadd.

JOHN T. MUIR was born in London and emigrated to Ireland. A writer of journalism, prose and drama, John's first love is poetry. Having received literary recognition in competitions in Ireland, Britain and Italy, he is also currently working on an epic novel. e-mail johntmuir@hotmail.com

ROBERT NAZARENE is Founding Editor of *Margie* / *The American Journal of Poetry*. Educated at the McDonough School of Business at Georgetown University, his poetry has appeared in *Beloit Poetry Journal*, *Boulevard*, *Crazyhorse*, *Green Mountains Review*, *New York Quarterly*, *The Oxford American*, *Ploughshares*, *Quarterly West*, and elsewhere. His first full-length collection, *CHURCH*, is forthcoming from IntuiT House in 2004.

NAOMI SHIHAB NYE is the author and/or editor of more than twenty volumes, including *19 Varieties of Gazelle: Poems of the Middle East* (Green Willow Books, 2002), and *Fuel* (Boa Editions, 1998). Nye lives in San Antonio.

RICHARD O'CONNELL lives in Richmond, Rhode Island. Collections of his poetry and translations include *Retro Worlds*, *Simulations*, *Voyages* and *The Bright Tower*, all published by the University of Salzburg Press. His poems have appeared in *The New Yorker*, *The Atlantic Monthly*, *The Formalist*, *National Review*, *Quarterly Review of Literature*, *Paris Review*, etc.

RENÉE ELLEN OLANDER's poems have appeared in *Controlled Burn*, *Verse and Universe*, *13th Moon*, *Sea of Voices*, *Isle of Story*, *HEArt*, *Amelia*, *Rhino*, and many others. She directs the Interdisciplinary Studies Dept. at Old Dominion U., in Norfolk, VA.

BARABRA PAPARAZZO is a writer from Conway, Massachusetts who has published poetry in *Atlanta Review*, *Wisconsin Review*, *River Oak Review*, *Peregrine* and others.

R. A. PAVOLDI is a Publications Production Manager with Excelsior College in Albany, NY. He lives in nearby Schenectady with his wife Teresa and their three children.

REBECCA HAZELTON PENNELL resides in Atlanta, GA. *Margie* is privileged to present her first published poem.

SIMON PERCHIK is an attorney whose poetry has appeared in *Partisan Review*, *The New Yorker* and elsewhere. A second printing of *Hands Collected*, a collection of 16 out-of-print books is now available from Pavement Saw Press. www.geocities.com/simonthepoet

ELLEN PERLESS grew up in New York, studied at Bard, and has returned to publishing after a long hiatus. Why she wound up in advertising instead of academia is too long a story to tell here. In that universe, which is surely a parallel one, she is best known for having written "Don't Hate Me Because I'm Beautiful" for Pantene, which has been immortalized on t-shirts and refrigerator magnets.

TERESA PFEIFER was born in Springfield, MA where she teaches English for the Vocational High School. Her work has been supported by the Massachusetts Cultural Council and has appeared in *Massachusetts Review*, *Verse*, *Poetry East*, and elsewhere.

JOHN PURSLEY III currently teaches poetry and literature at the University of Alabama, where he is also a poetry editor for *Black Warrior Review*. Recent poems have appeared or are forthcoming in *Aura Literary Review*, *GSU Review*, *Chelsea*, *Cold Mountain Review*, *The Distillery*, *New Delta Review*, *Notre Dame Review*, *West Branch* and *Yemassee*.

YOSEFA RAZ grew up in Jerusalem. She is a graduate of the UC Davis Creative Writing Program, where she received the Celeste Turner Wright Poetry Prize two years in a row. Her work has appeared or is forthcoming in various magazines including *ZYZZYVA* and *Glimmer Train*. Her book, *In Exchange for a Homeland*, is forthcoming from Swan Scythe Press this fall.

CHRISTINE RHEIN is a mechanical engineer turned stay-at-home mother and writer in Brighton, Michigan. Her recent poems appear or are forthcoming in *The Gettysburg Review*, *Atlanta Review*, *Literal Latté*, *The Sow's Ear Poetry Review*, and *The MacGuffin*. In 2002, she was awarded a writer's conference scholarship from AWP.

SUZANNE RHODENBAUGH's book, *Lick of Sense*, won the Marianne Moore Poetry Prize and was published by Helicon Nine Editions in 2002; it was one of five finalists for the Kessler Award at S.U.N.Y.-Binghamton, for the best poetry book published the previous year for a poet over forty. Her poems, essays, and articles have appeared in *The American Scholar*, *Hudson Review*, *New England Review* and other magazines.

SUZANNE RICHARDSON recently graduated from Princeton University, and is on her way to Washington University of St. Louis where she will pursue a Masters of Fine Arts degree. A Havre, Montana native, Suzanne has been writing poetry for ten years.

JAY ROGOFF's poetry has appeared in *The Paris Review*, *The Progressive*, *Salmagundi*, *The Southern Review*, *The Texas Review*, and elsewhere. His latest volume, *How We Came to Stand on That Shore*, is new from River City Publishing.

MICHAEL SALCMAN is a physician, brain scientist and essayist on the visual arts. He was professor and chairman of the department of neurosurgery at the University of Maryland and currently serves as president of the Contemporary Museum of Baltimore. His poems have appeared in *Raritan*, *Notre Dame Review*, *Harvard Review*, *Barrow Street*, *North Dakota Quarterly*, and elsewhere.

DAVID SALNER has been a longtime supporter of protests against police brutality. His poems have appeared in *Threepenny Review*, *5AM*, and *Washington Square*. His first collection, *The Chosen*, was published by Pudding House in 2002.

CINDY SAVETT received her BA from the University of Pennsylvania. She lives in the Philadelphia area with her family and has recently finished her first manuscript.

LON SCHNEIDER's poems, stories, and essays have appeared in *Mid-America Poetry Review*, *Rattle*, *Blue Satellite* and *Pearl*. Mr. Schneider, graduated from Horton Watkins High School in St. Louis, a classmate of Marjorie J. Wilson.

PETER SERCHUK is the author of the poetry collection, *Waiting for Poppa at Smithtown Diner* (University of Illinois Press). His poetry has appeared in *American Poetry Review*, *Poetry*, *North American Review*, *Mid-American Review*, *Mississippi Review*, and elsewhere.

JACQUELYN SHAH has a poetry M.F.A. from the University of Houston, where she is a teaching assistant. In 2004 she hopes to complete her Ph.D. in English literature and creative writing. New work is forthcoming in *The Texas Review*.

KATHLEEN SHEEDER teaches creative writing and high-school English in suburban Philadelphia. She is a former co-editor of *The American Poetry Review*.

DEREK SHEFFIELD won *North American Review's* 2003 James Hearst Poetry Award judged by Li-Young Lee. His chapbook, *A Mouthpiece of Thumbs* (Blue Begonia Press), is out and about, and his interview of William Stafford's family, "Talking Recklessly," appeared in *Seattle Review* (Spring 2003).

FLOYD SKLOOT's poems have appeared in or are forthcoming in *The Atlantic Monthly*, *Harper's*, *Poetry*, *Sewanee Review*, *Hudson Review*, *The Georgia Review*, *Southern Review*, *Boulevard*, *Iowa Review* and elsewhere. He was awarded the Emily Clark Balch Prize in Poetry for 2000 from *The Virginia Quarterly Review* and a poem has appeared in *The Best Spiritual Writing 2001*. His second collection of poems, *The Evening Light* (Story Line Press) won the 2001 Oregon Book Award, judged by Maxine Kumin. His third collection of poems, *The Fiddler's Trance* (Bucknell University Press), appeared in fall of 2001.

TOM SMITH is recently retired from Castleton State College, Professor Emeritus. He is the author of one novel and numerous volumes of poetry. Since 1959 his work has appeared widely in such magazines as *Iowa Review*, *New York Quarterly*, *The American Scholar*, *Virginia Quarterly Review*, and elsewhere.

KATHERINE SONIAT *New Poems* is forthcoming from Sarabande Books in April 2003. Her most recent book is *Ode to the Cold War: Poems New & Selected*, also from Sarabande. Recent poems appear or are forthcoming in *The Yale Review*, *Raritan*, *The Sewanee Review*, *Quarterly West*, and *Poetry*, among others. She is a recipient of an NEA Poetry Fellowship and her work has been featured on four occasions in *The Best American Poetry* annual volumes.

GARY SOTO is the author of twenty-five books for adults and young people. His most recent books include the children's biography *A Hero for Everyone: the Story of Cesar Chavez* (Simon and Schuster, 2003) and the adult novel *Amnesia in a Republican County* (University of New Mexico Press, 2003). His young-adult novel *The Afterlife* is due from Harcourt in spring 2004. He lives in Berkeley.

MARCELLA SPRUCE's poetry, essays, and short stories have appeared in *Literal Latté*, *The Anthology of New England Writers 1999*, *Compass Rose*, *The New York Times*, *Education Week*, *Reflections on Maine*, and *The Larcom Review*. She lives in Portsmouth, New Hampshire.

KAREN STANISLAW earned her B.A. from Sarah Lawrence College, and an M.A. from New York University's Gallatin School—the core of her thesis—a theatrical presentation of her poems at the WestBeth Theatre in NYC. She has also performed her work at the Teatro Santa Catarina in Mexico City. These poems represent her first publication of poetry.

S. ASHER SUND lives in Portland, Oregon. His fiction and poetry have been published in *Willow Springs*, *The Comstock Review*, *The Briar Cliff Review*, and *Square Lake*, among others. He received his M.F.A. from Eastern Washington University.

EMILY SUNDERLAND teaches high school English in Los Angeles, CA, where she lives. She graduated from Southern Connecticut State University with a major in English and a concentration in creative writing. Her poems have appeared in *Slipstream* and the *New Zoo Poetry Review*. She is currently working on a collection of short stories.

KIRK SWEARINGEN co-founded, with George Fortier, *The Project,* a poet's collective. A poem, "Lincoln's Mirror," appeared recently in *The Edge City Review.* He lives in Webster Groves, MO., with his wife and two daughters.

TONI THOMAS is a poet and sculptor. She holds an M.F.A. in Creative Writing and an MA in Counseling Psychology. She currently teaches at Marylhurst University and has worked as a children's art teacher, sales clerk, social worker, travel writer, on an assembly line in a paper box factory, and in marketing for a major corporation.

ALISON TOWNSEND's poetry has appeared in *Crazyhorse, New Letters, The Southern Review, Prairie Schooner, RATTLE,* and many other magazines. Her work has been widely anthologized. Her first full-length collection, *The Blue Dress: Poems and Prose Poems,* is new from White Pine Press. She lives near Madison, Wisconsin.

ANNA R. TREBORZE is a member of The Order of The Sisters of Saint-Gilles, located in the Quathlamba mountain range, Cape of Good Hope, South Africa. Sister Anna serves as Ethics & Policy Advisor to *Margie / The American Journal of Poetry.* These are her first published works of poetry.

ARLENE TRIBBIA has had poetry published in *The Evansville Review.* She lives in Palm Harbor, Florida where she's working on a novel, *How to Grow A Human Heart.*

PETRA UHRIG is a poet living in Saratoga Springs, New York. In a previous life, she was a bookkeeper, secretary, and university bureaucrat. Her interests include feminist-anarchist history, in particular the life of the anarchist poet Voltairine de Cleyre. Petra holds a degree in English from Montana State University. She was born in Germany and immigrated to the United States in 1963 at the age of six. These are her first poems published.

SALLY VAN DOREN's poetry has appeared or is due to appear in a number of quarterlies, among them *Colorado Review, Larcom Review,* and *River King Poetry Supplement.* She holds an M.F.A. in Creative Writing from the University of Missouri-St. Louis and a B.A. in Comparative Literature from Princeton University.

MELISSA J. VARNAVAS is a journalist and poet based in Beverly, Massachusetts. A member of the North Shore Poets Forum and the Massachusetts State Poetry Society, her work focuses on nature and family.

351

REETIKA VAZIRANI was the author of *World Hotel* (Copper Canyon 2002), and *White Elephants* (Beacon 1996). She had recently joined the Creative Writing Program at Emory University. We at the review were saddened to learn of her passing, in July of this year.

DAVID WAGONER has published seventeen books of poems, most recently *The House of Song* (Univ. of Illinois Press, 2002), and ten novels, one of which, *The Escape Artist*, was made into a movie by Francis Ford Coppola. He won the Lilly Prize in 1991, has been nominated twice for the National Book Award, and has won the Zabel Prize, the Blumenthal-Leviton-Blonder Prize, the Eunice Tietjens Prize, the English-Speaking Union Prize, the Levinson Prize, and the Union League Prize of *Poetry* (Chicago), and the William Stafford Memorial Award from the Pacific Northwest Booksellers. He was a chancellor of the Academy of American Poets for 23 years. He has taught at the University of Washington since 1954 and was the editor of *Poetry Northwest* till its end in 2002.

ANNE WALDMAN is a poet and teacher. Together with Allen Ginsberg, Ms. Waldman worked to form the Jack Kerouac School of Disembodied Poetics at Naropa Institute in Boulder, Colorado. She is the author of numerous volumes of poetry including, *Kill or Cure* (Penguin Poets) and *Iovis* (Coffee House Press). Ms. Waldman was featured in Bob Dylan's experimental film 'Renaldo and Clara'.

NICOLE WALKER is currently pursuing her Ph.D. at the University of Utah. She has published most recently in *New American Writing* and *Barrow Street* and won the Larry Levis prize (the little one, not the big one). In addition to teaching at the university, she hosts visiting writers and is poetry editor for *Quarterly West*.

DANEEN WARDROP's poetry has appeared or is forthcoming in *TriQuarterly*, *Michigan Quarterly Review*, *Seneca Review*, *Beloit Poetry Journal*, *Epoch*, and elsewhere. She is the author of two books of criticism, including *Emily Dickinson's Gothic* (University of Iowa Press). She teaches at Western Michigan University.

ELLEN WEHLE is a performance poet who reads at colleges and bookstores: "having a live audience helps winnow out the weaker poems." Upcoming publications include *Cream City Review*, *Slate*, *Nassau Review*, *FIELD*, and *Terra Incognita*.

MIKE WHITE, originally from Montreal, currently lives in Salt Lake City where he is enrolled in the doctoral creative writing program at the University of Utah. He also works as an editorial assistant at *Quarterly*

West. His poems have appeared or are forthcoming in *Tar River Poetry*, *West Branch*, *Poet Lore*, *The Comstock Review*, *River Oak Review* and *Pottersfield Portfolio*.

CATHERINE WING lives in Seattle where she is completing her M.F.A. at the University of Washington. Her work has appeared in *Tinfish*, *Fine Madness*, and *Hubbub*.

JONAH WINTER, whose poem *Sestina: Bob* was selected for the 2001 Pushcart Anthology, has published a book of poems, *MAINE*, selected by David Lehman for the 2002 Slope Editions Book Prize. He currently teaches llama repair at George Mason University.

AMANDA KATERI WISNIEWSKI is a Sayreville, NJ native. In May 2002, she earned her Bachelor of Science in Marine Science and a minor in Writing from The Richard Stockton College of New Jersey. She has received the Jeanette Gottlieb Award for Poetry in 2001 and 2002, and an Honorable Mention for the R.J. Corradino Award for Love Poetry in 2002. She will begin attending Sarah Lawrence College in September 2003 to pursue her M.F.A. in Creative Writing; Poetry. This is her first published work.

JOSEPH P. WOOD is on the faculty of both the University of Arizona and Pima Community College; his poems have appeared in *Gulf Coast*, *Passages North*, *Madison Review*, *Sycamore Review*, and elsewhere. He lives with his wife in Tucson, Arizona.

LAURA WRIGHT studies English at Baldwin-Wallace College in Berea, Ohio, where she serves as the 2003-04 editor of the college's art and literary magazine. Her poems have appeared in *Lynx Eye*, and she intends to pursue graduate studies in creative writing upon graduation.

Thank God
for Everything

Grateful appreciation is expressed to our many subscribers, contributors, advertisers, and friends of the review; and to Feed the Children, contest beneficiary of The Marjorie J. Wilson Award; and to the members and board of The St. Louis Poetry Center. Special thanks to Mr. Robert Pinsky for his great kindness and generosity.

The Robert E. Lee & Ruth I. Wilson

POETRY BOOK

DEADLINE: JANUARY 15, 2004

CONTEST

First Prize: $2,000

& Publication of the Winning Book

Finalist Judge: DARA WIER

*Author of eight books of poetry & winner of grants from the
Guggenheim Foundation & the National Endowment for the Arts*

ENTRY GUIDELINES: 1. Open to all writers,
writing in English. Manuscripts must be typed, single or double-
spaced, and consecutively numbered. Submit between 48-64 pgs.
of poetry. Clear photocopies are acceptable. 2. Include a cover
page (with author's name, address, phone & title of manuscript) &
a title page (with no biographical information.) Please include an
acknowledgements page listing poems previously published in
periodicals. 3. **Include an entry fee check for $25 payable to
MARGIE, Inc.** for each manuscript submitted. 4. Please include
a self-addressed stamped envelope (SASE) to receive notification
of contest results. No manuscripts can be returned. All manuscripts will be considered for publication. 5. **Mail entries to:**
IntuiT House, c/o MARGIE, POST OFFICE BOX 250,
CHESTERFIELD, MO 63006-0250

"Only the Strong*est* Survive."

IntuiT House

an imprint of *Margie / The American Journal of Poetry*

"Strong Rx Medicine"

www.margiereview.com
Post Office Box 250   Chesterfield, MO 63006-0250

Now Available from Verse Press

Hat on a Pond
poems by Dara Wier

Paperback, $13
ISBN 0-9703672-6-0

Sweet Obsession

It's been eleven days since
I've seen the fox.
Why did you put a whiskbroom
In the suitcase?
From the inside of my face
To the almond-sized bone
Of the soul is a far cry.
Way too wet to hold onto.
I admired how a plain ribbon
Snake shifted into reverse.
Deep in the bottom of my purse
There's a silver knife
With calla lilies carved
On its case. My surface
Remains lily-free for now.
It's been twenty-two days
Since I've seen the fox.
What do you keep in your pocket,
The one where your fingers go
To tell our secrets to subatomic gods?
It's been nine years since
I've seen the fox.
Tiny, tiny, tiny, tiny fox.

HAT ON A POND

DARA WIER

Order online at www.versepress.org
Available to the trade from Small Press Distribution

357

The

Sewanee Review

*A beacon
for American letters
since 1892*

$24 per year • $29 outside U.S. • MasterCard and Visa accepted

735 University Avenue • Sewanee TN 37383 • 931-598-1246

NEW LETTERS

A Journal of Writing & Art

Consistency

Daniel Woodrell
Marilyn Hacker
Amiri Baraka
H. L. Hix
Robin Becker
Sherman Alexie
Naomi Shihab Nye
Quincy Troupe
Janet Burroway
Maxine Kumin
Jonathan Holden
Robert Stackhouse

Complexity . . .

It's amazing.

Join our family of subscribers:
$17 one year; $28 two years (4 / yr.)
University House
5101 Rockhill Road
University of Missouri-Kansas City
Kansas City, MO 64110

Multicultural Literary Explorers
Since 1975

RIVER STYX

MAGAZINE

*following the river
from mouth to source*

*Best American Poetry,
The Pushcart Prize: Best of The Small Presses,
Beacon Best Creative Writing by
Women and Men of All Colors,
and
New Stories From the South*

RAFAEL CAMPO • MARILYN HACKER
SHARON OLDS • LAWRENCE RAAB • RON KOERTGE
CATIE ROSEMURGY • ANDREW HUDGINS
TIMOTHY LIU • WILLIAM TROWBRIDGE
DAVID KIRBY • MARK JARMAN

RIVER STYX • 634 N. GRAND BLVD. • TWELFTH FLOOR • ST. LOUIS, MO 63103
$20/THREE ISSUES, $35/SIX ISSUES, $48/NINE ISSUES, $7/SINGLE

NAME _____

ADDRESS _____

CITY _____ STATE _____ ZIP _____

PLEIADES • PL

Coming Soon:
Wisława Szymborska
Katie Ford
Richard Foerster
Lisa Lubasch
Max Winter
Arielle Greenberg
Angie Estes
G. C. Waldrep
Aliki Barnstone
Chris Offutt
James Tate
Sarah Manguso
Jean Valentine
Nicholas Montemarano
Katherine Vaz
Jesse Lee Kercheval
Ander Monson
and many others

Special Feature—Christianity and Poetry
A symposium and new poems by
Fanny Howe, Eric Pankey, Scott Cairns,
Jennifer Atkinson, and Paul Mariani

An Interview with Carl Phillips

2002
Pushcart Prize
& *Best American Poetry*
2002 & 2003

New from Pleiades Press
THE GREEN GIRLS, poems by John Blair
Available through Louisiana State University Press
(800) 861-3477; $15.95 paper; ISBN 0-8071-2855-4

Forthcoming from Pleiades Press
LURE, poems by Nils Michals
Available this fall
through Louisiana State University Press
(800) 861-3477; $15.95 paper

PLEIADES: A JOURNAL OF NEW WRITING
& PLEIADES PRESS
Dept. of English/CMSU/Warrensburg, MO 64093
$6 per issue/$12 per year—www.cmsu.edu/englphil/pleiades

MARGIE

The American Journal of Poetry

The First Annual

"STRONG MEDICINE"

POETRY CONTEST

DEADLINE: OCT. 31, 2003 (Halloween)

First Prize: $1,000

for Best Poem & Publication in *MARGIE*

Second Prize: $200 Third Prize: $100

Finalist Judge: Russell Edson

GUIDELINES:

1. Submit up to three unpublished poems (60 line limit per poem). 2. Enclose a cover sheet with your name, address, phone & title of each poem. No names on poems. 3. Enclose a $13 entry fee payable to MARGIE. 4. Add'l. poems may be submitted for $3 each add'l. poem. 5. Simultaneous submissions are acceptable. 6. Submissions must be postmarked by October 31, 2003. All submissions will be considered for publication in MARGIE. 7. Submit entries to: MARGIE, PO BOX 250, CHESTER-FIELD, MO 63006-0250. Include an SASE for contest results. Only submit copies as poems will not be returned. Questions? Email us at: margiereview@aol.com

www.margiereview.com

MARGIE POB 250 CHESTERFIELD, MO 63006-0250